without my children

A MEMOIR

SONIA LAMARCHE

JOANNE FEDLER *media*

Copyright © 2022 by Sonia Lamarche

All rights reserved. No part of this publication may be reproduced, stored in a retrieval system or transmitted in any form or by any means, electronic or mechanical photocopying, recording or otherwise without the prior written permission of the author.

First published by Joanne Fedler Media, 2022.

www.joannefedler.com

Book design by Laura Boyle Design

Author photo by Richard Day (Rich Day Media)

Printed in Australia, UK and USA.

National Library of Australia Cataloguing-in Publication data:

ISBN (Paperback) 978-1-925842-36-4

ISBN (E-book) 978-1-925842-37-1

JOANNE FEDLER *media*

A Word from the Author

When I first set out to write my story six years ago, I didn't realize what a cathartic experience it would be. I thought I'd solely focus on what it has been like to live without my children for many years. I didn't expect to find myself diving into my upbringing and realizing how deeply intergenerational trauma has affected my life decisions. What I discovered was just how much my environment shaped me and how hard I have fought to break that mould. What came as a surprise was how telling my story has made space for unexpected healing and forgiveness.

During the depths of my postpartum depression, I saw an interview with Brooke Shields on *Oprah*. I sat mesmerized, listening to her speak candidly about what she'd been through after having her first daughter. For the first time, I felt as if someone not only understood me but had the words to explain what I was feeling. Reading her memoir *Down Came the Rain* saved me. Her words breathed life back into me and gave me the strength to speak up about what I was going through. I knew then that I would be okay; that I'd eventually form a bond with my new baby and I'd mend my relationship with my little boy. I knew I would come out of it stronger, and I promised myself I would not be shamed into silence.

To provide my loved ones with a level of privacy, I have changed names, some locations and other characteristics. However, I've been loyal to the experiences, growth, healing and hard-earned wisdom as they happened. The words laid bare on these pages are my truth. My hope is that they provide you, my reader, with the same safe haven that *Down Came the Rain* provided for me.

Sonia Lamarche,
March 2022

This book is dedicated to the real Aidan & Cassie
thank you for making me a mother

Chapters

Last Goodbye	1
Me	7
Bartender	15
Eighteen	19
Playing House	25
Wedding Bells	29
Blue-eyed Boy	33
Unexpected Gift	39
Family Secrets	49
Down Came The Rain	53
A Mother's Love	57
Happy Pills	61
Buster	67
Unfaithful	71
An End and a Beginning	77

The People We Lean On	85
Downsizing	91
Get Out	95
The Aftermath	105
Co-parenting Anxiety	113
The Arena	119
Mommy Always Leaves	125
One-Way Ticket	131
Truth or Lie	135
Turbulence	139
Long Goodbyes	143
The Park	147
All The Things That Are Lost	149
Eat, Drink and Be Married	153
Skype	157
Photographs	163
Zurich	167
Repeating Betrayals	175
Love Triangle	181
Changes	185
Silence	189
Positively Complicated	193
The Irony of Life	197
Houston Bound	205
(Un)Settled	209
Familiar Foe	213
Moving On	217
Acknowledgments	221
Author Biography	223

Last Goodbye

I'm early. I'm always early. The arrivals terminal is mostly empty. A few others, like me, are waiting for the international red-eyes to land. I haven't seen my son, Aidan, since Christmas—a little over six months. I've missed him terribly. It has been years since we've had a long stretch of time together, and I was thrilled when he agreed to come visit me in Zurich. I suggested he stay for three weeks.

'It'll give you time to get over the jet lag and really enjoy yourself.'

'Only two,' he'd said. 'I have hockey camps.'

We settled on seventeen days. Small victories. I've learned to hold them close to my heart.

Aidan is different with me when his dad is around. He is aloof and keeps his distance. He rarely shows me any affection. I get it. He's pledging allegiance to the parent who stayed. He's nothing if not loyal. Our relationship started its slow and steady decline years ago, when I made the unforgivable decision to leave his father.

Despite us having joint custody, scheduled visits became shorter or were cancelled altogether. Hugs became quick and cold, almost cursory. His gaze exuded contempt rather than softness. The first summer after I moved to Zurich with my new husband, Dustin, my daughter Cassie came to stay for two months. Aidan opted to not come at all. I was sad but reasoned that he was at an age where friends matter more than parents. And yet this summer, he's agreed to seventeen uninterrupted days with us. I can't help but think that this could be a turning point in our relationship. Maybe this is the beginning of a new chapter for us, where we communicate more easily and start to relax in each other's company again.

I check the board. His flight has landed. My palms are sweaty, my heart shaky. I try not to think about what it will be like to have him with me. I don't want to get excited. I'm not sure which Aidan will walk through those doors. I'm hoping for the funny, kind and gentle one.

Suddenly, I catch a glimpse of him walking through the arrivals gate. He's grown another couple of inches. He appears more like a man than a fifteen-year-old boy. His upper body has filled in and he looks muscular, his biceps visible as he holds the straps of his backpack. His dad insisted that he fly as an unaccompanied minor. Watching the tiny Filipino flight attendant leading him is comical. She barely reaches his chest. He looks more like her bodyguard than she his keeper. His eyes scan the arrivals area, his jaw clenching and unclenching until our eyes lock. A slow smile creeps onto his face. I notice his teeth are perfectly straight. He looks different without his braces, more mature. I sign the paperwork and the flight attendant hands him off to me.

'Can I get a hug, kiddo?' I ask.

He pulls me in, the top of my head under his chin. I hold him tightly. He doesn't fight me. I can smell the long journey on him. I'm reminded of when he was younger and how sweaty he would get from playing hockey. That sweet yet pungent smell would linger no matter how often I washed his jersey. A flood of memories comes crashing into my mind. As we walk across the terminal and make our way to the train station, I notice the small hairs above his upper lip. *I wonder if he's started shaving?* Aside from a slight stubble near his sideburns, his skin is smooth and soft-looking.

'You don't have a car?' he asks, looking at the trains leaving the platforms.

'Nope. Don't need it. The trams and trains get us everywhere.' I point to a train slowing down. 'This is us.'

We sit across from each other. He stares out the window, a grin dancing on his lips. 'This is kinda cool, actually.' He pauses as we come out of the tunnel. 'Oh wow, the buildings look so old.'

I tell him about the plans we've made for his stay. Travels around Switzerland, the Montreux Jazz Festival and a short daytrip to an amusement park in Germany. I keep glancing over, taking him all in. He's wearing the T-shirt I bought him on my last trip to Canada. His hair, long and flowy last I saw him, has been cut short on one side and slightly longer on the other. The modern style takes the emphasis off the cowlick in the front. It looks good on him. I marvel at the fact that I am actually going to have this time with him. My heart is full.

Our little Chihuahuas can't contain their excitement when we walk through the door. He's amazed that they remember him. He sits on the floor laughing as he tries to pet them. Blue is running laps all over the apartment, jumping on him, licking his face. Betty can't help but whimper every time he reaches out for her as she rolls onto her back for belly rubs. I watch, tears pooling in my eyes. Dustin puts his hand on my shoulder and squeezes. They've missed him, too. I show him the guest room. Cassie, who's already been with us for a few weeks, has agreed to sleep on the sofa bed in the living room while her brother visits. I watched her move her stuffed animals and favorite blanket and felt a pang of guilt, wishing we had designated rooms for each of them, like we did in Calgary.

The next day we pack a picnic and head down to the lake. We play UNO cards and reminisce about when they were younger. I recount stories of how Aidan would share his Hot Wheels cars with his baby sister, and she would end up throwing them at his head. They laugh when I tell them about the time I left them alone for a few minutes to come back and find that he had buried her with his stuffed animals, swearing she had asked for them. I have many stories from their birth up until they were six and eight years old. Then the memories start to slowly dry up.

For the first few days, we stick close to home, venturing out to roam the narrow streets through the old town. Cassie and I take him to our favorite shawarma place, and we eat on the steps by the church where I attend a meditation circle. We linger by the lake, and I buy them ice cream where we sit looking at the Swiss Alps in the distance. The weather is perfect, with a warm breeze and bright blue skies.

'I can't believe there's still snow on the mountains in August,' Aidan says.

'It reminds me of when we would go to Banff,' Cassie continues.

Sitting between them, my heart is bursting, and I want to freeze this moment.

We hike, catch trains and gondolas connecting us to various villages and old towns. We take a boat from Felsenegg to Luzern, where we wander through the cobblestone streets before settling on a lunch spot by the lake. At the Montreux Jazz festival, on the shore of Lake Geneva, we listen to Macy Gray and Tom Jones, swaying to the rhythm of the music. I can't stop smiling as I soak it all in. I agree to go on all of the rides at the amusement park in Germany, even though I'm terrified. I want to show him as much of Switzerland as I can in the short time he's with us, hoping it'll convince him to come back and explore neighboring countries.

Being together feels effortless and relaxed. Everyone gets along, without arguments or fights—it's peaceful. The time flies by. There is no surly teenage boy. He is the Aidan from my memories, seemingly untouched by the divorce poison. We talk about the easy and difficult stuff.

'I'm thinking about moving here,' Cassie, who has just turned thirteen, announces one night during happy hour.

'Well, if you're going to do it, now's the right time. Before you start high school,' Aidan responds. I'm not sure if he understands that she doesn't mean for just one year.

On the last night before they leave, we all get dressed up and take pictures on the terrace of our favourite Italian restaurant. We order white wine and let them each have a small glass. It's the European way. We talk and laugh and take more pictures. I smile through the heaviness of their upcoming departure weighing on my heart. Aidan acts silly while I film him on the tram ride back home.

Their trip ends too quickly, with the airport witnessing our goodbyes yet again.

'One more hug?' I ask. Cassie obliges. I hold her closely and kiss the top of her head. 'Love you.'

A slight pause. 'Love you, too. I'll text you when we land in Canada.'

I turn to Aidan and he opens his arms. My face buried in his chest, I whisper, 'I love you so much, A,' holding him tightly, not wanting to let go.

He pulls away, and looks me straight in the eyes. 'I had fun, Mom, but I'm never coming back.'

I smile, fighting back the tears, 'Don't be so sure, kiddo, maybe you'll decide to come back next summer.'

He shakes his head. 'No, I won't.'

The muffled drum of my heart is beating in my ears. I must not have heard correctly. I look up at him and he stands firmly, his gaze holding mine. I blink back my tears and, behind him, notice the gate agent walking towards us. It's time for them to board the plane. I press my face to the glass, watching them walk down the ramp and wave. I'm unable to hold back the sob that escapes my throat. And just like that, they are gone.

I wish I had known then that those would be the last words we would say to each other face to face. I might have done something differently—I don't know what, but I might have.

On the train home, I scroll through the pictures on my phone. Was he serious about never coming back? Why? A wave of sadness threatens to drown me. I watch the video I took of him on the tram the night we all got dressed up and went for that fancy dinner. I smile though tearful eyes. I freeze the video on his smiling face, his eyes directly looking into mine. He was happy, wasn't he? I thought we had reconnected and closed some of the gap. I believed we were finding each other again. I replay the memories on a loop.

In the four years since then, I've often wondered if he'd acted that way, knowing all he'd be leaving me with were the small morsels of those photos, videos and memories before he blocked me from his life for good.

Me

The notion that I would have children was planted in me at a young age. You grow up, meet the man of your dreams, get married and have babies. It seemed like a pretty simple formula to follow.

I am the youngest of three, the *baby*, except that I have never felt like a baby. From my earliest childhood memories, from 6 a.m. Monday to 6 p.m. Friday, there was always someone smaller I had to help care for. I loved inventing new games, making crafts and swimming with the younger kids. At pick-up, parents would comment what a great mother I would be to my own children someday.

The playroom in our basement had more toys than we needed, but none of them were truly ours; they were for all the kids to play with—including those at my mother's daycare. My new Barbie dolls were only mine for the day or so after I unwrapped them on the weekend, and then they were added to the pile of Barbies to be shared. Sharing was important, and I wanted to be good at it. Some of the daycare kids would bring toys from their homes and leave with them in the evening. I didn't understand why I couldn't keep my precious toys in my room, although I didn't dare say any of this out loud. I didn't want to be a brat, so instead, when I'd clean up the playroom, I'd hide my favorite toys under the staircase, where they wouldn't be found, and took them out to play on weekends.

•••

When I was four, a new baby arrived at the daycare. Eva was only six weeks old when my mom started babysitting her. She was the smallest human I'd ever seen. She had a full head of black hair, chubby cheeks, dark eyelashes and a button nose. She would crinkle her nose and purse her tiny lips when she was about to cry. Because I was a 'big girl' and 'Mom's helper,' I was allowed to touch her. None of the other kids had this privilege.

I only went to kindergarten for half-days, so my job was to watch the baby when she slept. My mom would lay her on the sofa in the special living room where no kids were allowed. This adult living room was off-limits even on weekends. There was an invisible line we didn't dare cross. I would stand with my toes barely touching the shaggy carpet while my dad sat in the rocking chair, smoking his pipe and reading the newspaper. If I was particularly well-behaved, he would sit me on his knee and rock me until I fell asleep. I used to love laying my head on his belly, the smell of his pipe sweet and sticky in my nose.

Baby Eva napped with pillows all around her to make sure she wouldn't fall off the sofa. I'd kneel down, tuck my chin in between two pillows and watch her sleep. I spent countless hours watching her little chest and belly rise and fall. I listened to the small noises she made while she slept, watched her eyelids flutter while she dreamt. And when her little arms would flail around, I'd poke my hand through and let her wrap her tiny fingers around mine. I became attuned to her movements and could tell ahead of time when she would start to whine or cry. I would stand up and very gently run my index finger up and down, from the curve of her nose to the hairline on her forehead. She would relax and go back into a deep sleep. She quickly became my favorite person. She was the little sister I'd always wanted, my very own human doll.

My parents planned their offspring with that careful four-year gap. 'It's easier to have a baby when the last born is self-sufficient and in school,' my mom would say. My sister, Lisa, eight years older, had curly red hair, green eyes and freckles. In comparison, I had poker-straight brown hair, brown eyes, a crooked nose and big ears. I wished I looked more like her.

As a teenager, I was so desperate to emulate her that for years I permed my hair and begged my parents to buy me colored contact lenses. She was strong-minded and independent, and rarely followed the rules. She often argued with my parents, defying my mother. She didn't have the same need to please I had. When I was ten years old, she left for college. We weren't close when I was growing up, but once I moved out of my parents' home, she became an important person in my life. I loved spending time with her and her two children. I knew I could turn to her whenever I felt as if I'd disappointed my parents. When I decided to quit university, she was the first person I told. She held me as I cried because my father had told me that if I didn't return to my studies, he would disown me (he eventually apologized and accepted my decision to pursue a different path). I knew her door was always open for me. She was one of my biggest supporters through my separation, always welcoming me and my kids into her home whenever I needed family.

My brother, four years older than me, has my dad's blue eyes and my mom's dark hair. He played ice hockey from a young age and was often away for practice, games and tournaments. He was quietly magnetic and became one of the popular kids in high school. Although he loved to torment me, as big brothers sometimes do, he was also protective of me. When boys were interested in me, he'd go out of his way to intimidate them, and in this way, I knew he cared about my safety and happiness.

My dad worked in a management position for the Canadian Parliament. He was responsible for the restaurants, souvenir shop and liquor store. He was always gone before I woke up because of the long commute to the city. In the evening, I'd look out the window, waiting for the van to pull up to the driveway. He'd get out and wave to the driver, and I'd run out to greet him. He would put down his black briefcase and scoop me up in his arms. He always helped with housework, gardening and chores. Most nights, he'd sit at the kitchen table and help me with my schoolwork. He was patient and always had time for his kids. Some of my favorite memories are of standing on his feet while we danced in the kitchen. He would twirl me around and I'd fall to the floor, giggling. He was the authoritarian of the home, and we all feared him. My mom knew that all she had to do was threaten to tell Dad we had misbehaved. I've never felt more shame than the few times in my life when my dad told me I'd disappointed him.

My mom ran a home daycare from the time my was sister was born. Before that, she worked in the kitchen of a nunnery in the city, preparing meals. The values of cleanliness, order and discipline were the pillars of our home. Even though it was not uncommon to have twelve to fifteen kids running in and out of the house on most days, the kitchen was clean, the carpets were vacuumed and the playroom was tidy. Everything had a place, and nothing was out of order. Mom took great care of herself and how she looked. She never left the house without her hair and makeup perfect. She was always the prettiest woman in the room. I enjoyed helping her, because she would praise me. I loved how her hand felt on the top of my head when she'd ruffle my hair and say those words: *My little helper. I can always count on my baby.* When she got a part-time job as a cashier at the local grocery store, my dad was not supportive. I overheard her tell him, 'I get lonely being with kids all day. I need to have adult interaction.' He told her to do what she pleased, but she didn't work there very long. As much as she wanted to have a life outside of our home that didn't involve raising young kids, she chose to keep my father happy. I used to lie at the top of the stairs and eavesdrop on their adult conversations. The fear and anticipation of getting caught made my tummy tingle. I learned early on that women are meant to put their desires aside in order to keep the peace at home. As much as my mom longed for social interaction, she could never put herself first. The needs of her husband and kids always took precedence over her own.

As a child, I wanted to marry someone just like my dad—a strong, hard-working, sturdy man who loved his wife and children and did his half of the parenting. I know my parents had their difficult years, with many hardships to overcome. One of the main reasons they stayed together was for the sake of us kids. Many parents of their generation made this same choice, to give their children a traditional family. It's not my place to say whether this was the right decision or not. All I know is that I never once doubted the profound love they had for me and my siblings.

It wasn't until much later in life that I understood the depth of love and respect they had for each other, too. They both made mistakes and sacrifices along the way. They hurt and got hurt. Their marriage wasn't perfect; no marriage ever is. This gives me some comfort when I look back on the mistakes I made in my first marriage. The difference is that my mom remains my dad's entire world, and they are each other's favorite person. As far as role models go, I couldn't have asked for two better ones.

In this relatively stable and happy home, I grew into a shy teenager who wasn't popular, athletic, nerdy or artsy in high school. I didn't make friends easily and so kept to myself.

In the summer months between grade school and high school, my body transformed into that of a woman. I suddenly had large breasts, long legs, hips and a soft belly. My mom told me to be mindful of how I acted around boys and not to 'entice them' with my newfound curves. I shrank, uncomfortable in my new body, trying my best to go unnoticed. I would keep my head down and walk faster when older teenage boys cat-called and whistled as I passed. I learned which hallways to avoid and steered clear of the cafeteria at lunchtime. I had a few close friends, and that was enough for me.

I rarely went out, preferring to just stay home on weekends. In tenth grade, my friend persuaded me to go to a party with her. All the cool kids would be there, she said. People brought tents to stay overnight and avoid driving drunk. Because my parents knew I was responsible, they agreed to let me take the car overnight. After a few hours, I went looking for my friend. She was in our tent with her boyfriend and asked if I could find somewhere else to sleep. Annoyed, I rolled my eyes. I had started walking to my car when a boy I had a crush on caught up to me.

'Hey—I have extra space and blankets in my tent, if you want. It's probably better than sleeping in your car.' He tilted his head and smiled. 'Promise I'll be a gentleman.' Kids were still huddled around the fire, spilling beer and shouting over the boom box playing music.

'Sure, thanks,' I said, wondering if anyone would notice us.

∙ ∙ ∙

I woke the next morning as the sun was rising, the dawn light basking everything in a gold halo. I was facing him and watched as he slept, his lips slightly parted. His black hair lay across his forehead, long eyelashes brushing up onto his flushed and rosy cheeks. I traced the scar on his upper lip with my finger. He opened his eyes and smiled. In that perfect morning light, I wanted to feel his lips on mine. I moved in closer and kissed him. He moaned and kissed me back. We unzipped our sleeping bags and he took off his sweater. I marveled at his strong chest and bronzed torso. He helped take my sweater off and gently caressed my breasts over my bra. He kissed my neck, cheeks, eyes, mouth—and I melted. I felt his erection on my thigh and reached for it. He reached down to unzip my jeans, and I heard voices outside our tent. I placed my hand on his.

'We should stop—they might hear us,' I said, pointing to the shadows on the tent.

'Okay.' He gave me a peck on the cheek and pulled his sweater back on. I fumbled with mine as he unzipped the tent and walked out.

He joined his friends sitting around a newly lit campfire. I followed and sat next to him on a rock and put my head on his shoulder. He stiffened and stood up quickly to throw twigs in the fire. Embarrassed, I went to my friend's tent at the far end of the lot. I called out that I was heading home, not caring if she heard me. She could find a ride back. I looked over at him before getting into my car and saw a few of the guys patting his back. All I could think, driving away, was, *Thank God I didn't sleep with him.*

∙ ∙ ∙

I dreaded having to go past his locker at school on Monday morning. I kept my eyes down and hurried, trying to go unnoticed. All the boys laughed when I walked by. My friend from the party was leaning on my locker. 'I didn't think you had it in you,' she said, smirking.

'Had what?' I asked.

'Don't play coy with me. I know you guys banged. Everyone at the party saw you go into his tent. And he told his buddies that you're very good with your mouth.'

I felt the heat rise from my belly to my cheeks. I thought I was going to be sick. I glanced over at him. He nodded, with a snide look on his face, before walking away with his friends.

'I didn't sleep with him. We kissed. That's it.' I slammed my locker door.

She shrugged and said, 'Look, it's no big deal. We've all done it. Don't be weird about this.'

Like all things in high school, eventually people moved on to some other drama. Unfortunately, the reputation that I was an 'easy lay' followed me for the next two years. The assumption that I had slept with someone I wasn't dating emboldened other guys to corner me, comment on my body or grope me as I walked by. They assumed that if they asked me out, I'd sleep with them. I was slut-shamed by guys and girls who didn't know me personally, based on a story my crush had fabricated. It didn't matter that I was still a virgin. My mother's words reminding me not to 'entice' boys with my newfound curves rang in my ears with every slap on the ass I got walking to my classrooms. It's not that I was 'saving' myself, or that I didn't want to have sex. But I wanted my first time to be with someone I liked; I wanted that moment to be special. I hoped for gentle kisses and lingering touches. Giggles and awkwardness, something to remember fondly later in life.

But this tainted experience made me wonder if this would remain just a romantic fantasy.

Bartender

'Check out the guy behind the bar—I'd tap that,' my roommate Judith said, pointing to the bartender.

He had dark hair, thick eyebrows and a cigarette hanging out of the corner of his mouth as he passed drinks down the bar. He wore terrible baggy jeans with his black STAFF T-shirt tucked in. He noticed me staring and gave a nod. A few minutes later, a waitress dropped off two tequila shots.

'On the house,' she shouted, over the blaring music. I turned to thank her, but she was gone. I looked over at the bar, and the bartender gave a small smile before disappearing behind a wall of thirsty customers.

After last call for drinks was announced, Judith and I sidled up to the bar to thank him properly. We chatted. He had this really cute, lopsided way of smiling, like one side of his mouth couldn't quite catch up to the rest of the smile. He had gorgeous hazel eyes that lit up when he laughed, and I suddenly saw what Judith did. There was a dark and broody handsomeness about him.

We made it a point to chat to him every time we went to the bar, and one night, he invited us out for breakfast with the rest of the bar staff. The more I got to know Jason, the more I liked him. We went on a few dates, but neither of us wanted anything serious. I'd had a bad experience in a relationship before him, and I wasn't ready to start something new. Most of our time was either spent at the bar where he worked or cuddled up on the sofa watching movies. Because he was always around people and loud music, he preferred quiet nights in.

The first time we had sex, I cried. Each thrust sent searing pain through my body. I closed my eyes and reminded myself that this was my decision.

He held me afterwards and said that it meant a lot that I chose to give him my virginity.

'My last girlfriend also cried the first time we slept together,' he said, kissing the top of my head.

I didn't correct him.

Sexual intimacy never became a big part of our relationship, but we continued to see each other.

I met his family a few months later. I already knew his brother Theo, because he worked at the bar too. He and Jason shared a car so they were a package deal. I immediately loved his mom, who was full of life and kindness. His father was loud and boisterous and liked the idea that Jason was dating a French girl. His little sister took a while to warm up to me. Jason was her favorite brother, and she was territorial. I only met his older sister several months later. We took a trip to Sudbury to spend a few days with her and her new husband.

We spent a lot of time at his parents' house, and so his mom and I became close. Our bond grew as time went by. She enjoyed teaching me new recipes, and I loved helping her in the kitchen. At Christmas, we baked and made chocolates for the whole family. She was warm and welcoming, and I found it easy to talk to her. She was always willing to help me out with any home project I took on.

While I still had reservations about whether I could see myself spending the rest of my life with Jason, our relationship was growing and evolving. Some of his behaviors bothered me, but I told myself that, over time, he could change. He wasn't always kind to his mom. At first, I'd call him out on it. I wondered if the disrespect he displayed towards her when he was upset would eventually transfer to me. His bursts of anger startled me. His tendency to curse when he'd get mad disturbed me. But as much as his words could hurt, it was his cold silences that tore me apart. I tried hard not to make him angry, because I hated the way he could so easily withhold love and affection.

Looking back, I can see how desperate I was to be loved. I wanted to belong somewhere and to someone. Jason would often say that he loved my 'innocence and lack of refinement.' He found it charming that I was 'a rough gem.'

And so, without realizing it, I made myself smaller; I left parts of me behind and became the demure, innocent girl I thought he could love.

Eighteen

I looked at the pregnancy test in my hand, trying to convince myself that it was better to know than to pretend that my period wasn't late. I had to be sure before I told him. Maybe I wouldn't have to tell him at all. I read the instructions a second time; heaven forbid I did this wrong and the test be positive.

I peed on both sticks, placed them by the sink and waited. I glanced down, saw a faint line, decided they were both negative, wrapped them in toilet paper and buried them at the bottom of the garbage bin. Washing my hands, I looked at my reflection in the mirror. I needed to be sure. I dug the tests back out of the bin. Even before unwrapping them, I knew. They both had two pink lines. My gaze drifted to my stomach. I placed a hand on it, wondering if this was really happening. How could I be pregnant? I didn't *feel* pregnant. I sat on the bathroom floor with my head in my hands. Thoughts and images flooded my mind. *A baby?* I wasn't ready to be a mother. I wasn't ready to take on the responsibility of a child. I stood up and shoved the tests back to the bottom of the bin. I splashed cold water on my face and shook my head in the mirror. 'No, I can't do this,' I whispered to myself.

My mom was seventeen when she married my dad, a few months short of her eighteenth birthday. She became pregnant that same year and had my sister at nineteen. Women married and had children young at that time.

My sister went away to college shortly after she turned seventeen. She wanted to become a nurse. She met someone, got pregnant and decided to quit nursing school. I remember her calling to let my parents know about her decision. My mom was visibly shaken and collapsed into my dad's arms as she told him their daughter was quitting college two months shy of graduation.

'She's pregnant,' she'd said, weeping. The tears that flowed over the next several months were etched into my young mind.

I had never wanted to make the same mistake, yet here I was—eighteen and pregnant.

I didn't know if I should tell Jason or not. I had no idea how he'd react.

•••

I settled on telling him that night, when he came over after his shift at the bar. All I knew was that I was in no way ready to be a mother. I'd made my decision and was not having this baby. I didn't have the financial means to raise a child, nor did I have the time or courage. I was a college student working full-time and could barely afford to take care of myself.

I spent the day reminding myself of all the hardship my sister had gone through when she had her son. Even though I was only fourteen at the time, I saw how the financial hurdles, worries about finding adequate housing, and sleepless nights took their toll on her. Having a baby meant that I would be responsible for a life other than my own, and I wasn't ready for that level of responsibility. I was also terrified of disappointing my parents.

I was sitting on the sofa in the dark when he came in a little after 4 a.m. Usually, he would let himself into the apartment and crawl into my bed, where I'd be fast asleep, but not tonight. He sat at the other end of the sofa and looked at me without saying a word.

EIGHTEEN

'I'm pregnant.' I paused. 'I'm not keeping it.' Still nothing. No words, no movement. He slowly rubbed his face with both his hands.

'I thought you were on the pill.'

'I am on the pill.' Even in the dark, I could feel his eyes searching me.

'You sure you don't want to keep it?'

I nodded. 'One hundred percent sure.'

He moved closer and wrapped his arms around me. 'It's gonna be okay,' he whispered. I wasn't sure who he was trying to convince.

•••

The morning of the termination, he drove me to the clinic. He wasn't allowed to stay after I checked in. I was taken to a small room, where I was shown a detailed video of the procedure I was about to undergo. I was left alone with my thoughts for another hour or so before being wheeled to the operating room. I kept reminding myself that I had made the right decision.

An hour later, I was dressed and was taken to the main area, where Jason was waiting. His brother was sitting next to him. *I guess our little secret isn't a secret anymore.* We rode back to my apartment in complete silence. He drove, his brother sat in the front, and I sat in the back. Each bump in the road sent a searing pain through my pelvis, reminding me that there was no longer a fetus growing in my uterus.

'Did you want to come up?' I asked before getting out of the car.

'I can't. I have to drive Theo home and get ready for my shift at the bar.'

I nodded.

I walked up the stairs to my apartment, leaned my head against the door and took a deep breath before opening it. My roommate, Judith, was sitting on the sofa with a bowl of ice cream, watching TV. She got up and pulled me in for a hug. The wave of sadness was too big to keep at bay. I lay on the sofa with my head in her lap; she gently stroked my hair, and I cried until I had no tears left.

•••

The dream still haunts me. It doesn't come as often now, but I can still count on it showing up when I am least expecting it. I am sitting on a bench at the park, and there is a small boy on the swing set. He's waving to me. I look around and see that he is here alone. I stand and make my way to him slowly. He asks if I can push him.

His face is blurry, but I can see his curly, dark hair perfectly. I push and he giggles and shrieks, begging me to push harder and higher. I ask where his mommy is and he looks at me with a knowing smile. His face comes into focus, and I realize that he is mine. I am his mother. He is the baby I did not birth. He is the pregnancy I chose to terminate.

I kneel before him, hot tears running down my cheeks. I tell him I am so sorry and beg for his forgiveness. He wipes away my tears with his small hand. I watch him stand and slowly walk away until he disappears. I am still kneeling in the sand, crying, and he is gone. To this day, whenever I find myself by a swing-set at a park, I feel his presence. I can almost hear the whispers of his giggles. Although he is physically absent, to me, he is always present.

•••

In the months that followed the termination, I tried opening up to Jason about how I felt. Whenever I'd bring it up, he'd change the subject, telling me that there was no point in rehashing the past.

'What's done is done,' he'd say.

And while I knew that talking about it wouldn't change anything, I needed him to hear me out, maybe give me reassurances that everything would be okay. I wanted him to tell me that I was not a horrible person for terminating the pregnancy. I wanted him to hold me tightly and grieve with me, or at least allow space for my grief in our relationship. I had hoped he would be more sympathetic to the physical and emotional trauma I'd gone through. I suppose I wanted to talk about the impact this experience had on him as well. I had made the decision to terminate the pregnancy before I even told him about it, but I needed him to acknowledge that this had been a difficult choice. We had only been seriously dating for four months when I became pregnant. Although pregnancy affects men and women differently, I had hoped we could gain some closeness and closure from this by talking it through. I had never thought of him as a father, let alone the father to my child. But I couldn't understand how he could just put this life event behind him, as though I'd never been carrying his child to begin with.

Like so many other times in my life, I felt completely alone in my sadness and grief. But I did what I had always done—I put my pain and sorrow in a box and buried it deep within the dark spaces of my body. I forced myself to be grateful for the positives in my life and kept moving forward. Looking back was too painful, so I convinced myself that the times ahead would be brighter.

While I had decided to terminate the pregnancy, I still found it hard to find closure and properly allow myself the time to mourn what might have been. I did not share my pregnancy and termination with my family, for fear of being shamed. I felt immense guilt and embarrassment that I had gotten pregnant to begin with. I thought I was being safe and responsible by using birth control. In pushing away my thoughts and feelings around this decision, I dissociated from the grieving part of myself. It wasn't until many years later, when I allowed myself to revisit this part of me, that I was able to begin to heal from this loss.

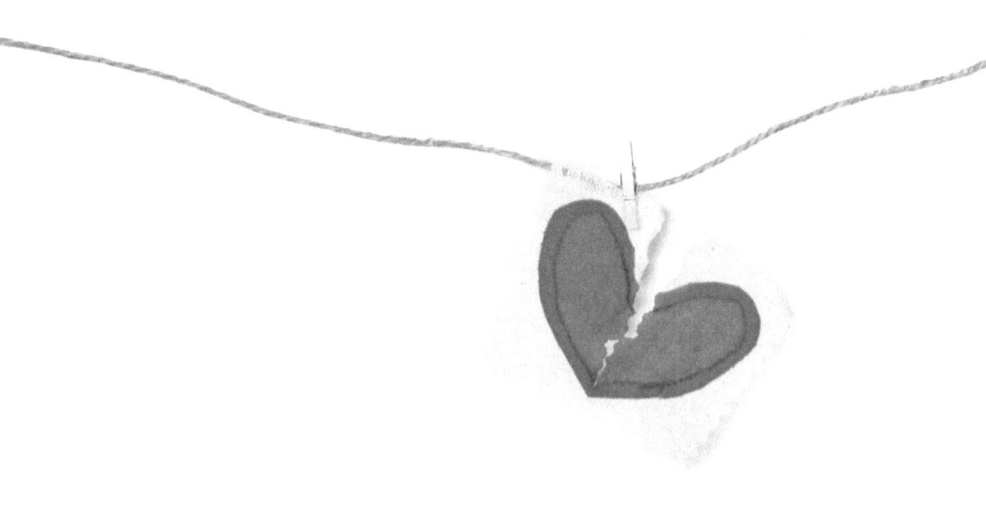

Playing House

Jason and I had been seeing each other for eight months when we took our first trip together. Judith and I had been arguing a lot, so I was happy to get away. She and I had recently moved into a new apartment closer to downtown, which made commuting to work and school easier. All we could afford was a one-bedroom, which was fine, except for when Jason stayed over.

Before he and I started dating, I had spent all of my free time with Judith. After Jason arrived in my life, she often complained that I no longer had time for her. I told her she was being clingy, and she told me I was being selfish. We started ignoring each other when we were both at home. Nonetheless, I never expected what was about to happen. It was pretty late when Jason and I pulled up in front of the complex. I looked up and saw that our apartment was completely dark and the curtains were closed.

Weird, I thought, *she should be back from work by now.*

I took my bag from the trunk of Jason's car and kissed him goodbye.

After almost a week together, I was ready for a little space. 'I'll walk you up,' he said.

'I'm good. I'll just wave to you from the window so you know I'm in.'

'No, I'd rather walk you up,' he insisted.

I opened the door, turned on the lights and realized that the apartment was completely empty. It took a minute for my mind to process what I was seeing. I pulled off a yellow Post-it note that had been left on the wall.

I've moved out, Judith xoxo.

His phone rang and I heard him say, 'Hey Theo,' while I walked towards the bedroom. I sat on my bed and looked at my clothes hanging in the closet. She had taken all of my things out of our shared dresser and thrown them on the ground, next to the lamp base that no longer had a lampshade or a lightbulb. I heard muffled voices and walked back to the doorway, where Theo was standing, and handed him the note. I found it odd that he didn't seem surprised.

He then told me that Judith had called him after she and her family had packed up the apartment. They had become friends over the months that Jason had been dating, because the four of us often hung out together. Jason avoided my gaze by looking at his feet.

'I wanted to tell you, Sonia,' Theo said. 'Jason thought it would be better to wait until you got back.'

I turned to Jason. 'You knew that she moved out and you didn't tell me? Why?' I could feel my cheeks burning up.

He looked guilty. 'I don't know. I just didn't want it to ruin our trip. I figured it didn't matter anyway. She'd still be gone. It's not like you could've stopped her.'

'Wow. Not cool. You should have told me right away. Instead, I come back to an empty apartment and a fucking Post-it on the wall,' I said, throwing the sticky-note on the ground.

I stomped to the bathroom, slamming the door behind me. There was a slight knock. 'Sonia, open the door. Come on, let's talk about this.'

I sat on the edge of the tub and rubbed my face in my hands. 'Go home. I'm tired and I don't want to fight with you right now.'

He drummed his fingers on the door. 'Okay, I'll go.'

Why did these men think that it was okay to keep this information from me? Why was Jason more concerned about not ruining our trip than he was about letting me return to an empty apartment? I knew that Jason and Theo had violated my boundaries, but instead of standing up for myself, I chose to stay quiet. My life was about to be heavily impacted by Judith moving out, and I had no idea what I was going to do now.

I was lying in the dark, staring at the ceiling, when I heard my phone ding.

1 new message from Jason: *Maybe I could move in?*
It hadn't taken him long.

•••

I wasn't sure I was ready for us to live together. But I couldn't afford the apartment on my own, and I still had eight months on the lease. *He's sleeping here most nights as it is; maybe he should pay half the rent,* I reasoned. This would also mean Theo would no longer be a guaranteed third wheel in our relationship, because Jason could walk to the bar from my apartment instead of relying on him for rides. Maybe we would have more time on our own to get to know each other better.

Let's talk tomorrow, I texted back.

A week later, Jason moved in. Because I worked days and he worked nights, we often only crossed paths in the hallway. We'd joke that we were more like roommates than lovers, sharing spaces instead of a life. I didn't mind this routine. I cherished still being able to have my freedom and alone-time.

On the rare nights that we were together, we mostly stayed in, watched movies and cuddled on the sofa. We hardly ever ate meals together, but when we did there was an unspoken understanding that, as the woman, I was responsible for the cooking and cleaning. I once made the mistake of saying that I enjoyed washing the dishes because the warm water thawed my always-cold hands. He took this to mean that I would always do the dishes and often left the kitchen a mess for me to clean up when I got home. It bothered me that he didn't do his share of household chores. I'd ask him to do more, but he would blame his inability to help out on his work schedule.

Feeling like a nag, I eventually stopped asking.

He loved snuggling in bed, wrapping his body completely around mine. I didn't, but I obliged. Most nights, he would wake me by moving my sleeping body around to get himself comfortable. It made me feel smothered. I didn't like being held so tightly that I couldn't move. I felt trapped, like a doll or stuffed animal a person clings to while they sleep. I once told him that I'd prefer if he didn't move me when he came to bed.

'I have a hard time falling back to sleep,' I said. He threw the covers off and stood, grabbing his pillow and a blanket.

'Fine, then, I'll just sleep on the sofa and move to the bedroom when you leave for work.'

I sighed. 'That's not what I meant. Come to bed, it's fine. Please?' I begged.

This was the tenor of our intimacy. Sometimes I wondered what long-term romantic love was meant to feel like and told myself that I was lucky to have someone care for me the way he did. I enjoyed the time we spent with his family, where I felt a deep sense of belonging and connection. I wasn't ready to give that up.

With hindsight, I see how, from the very beginning of our relationship, I changed aspects of myself to become who I thought he wanted me to be. To avoid tension, I stopped having opinions or disagreeing with him. I never considered both how detrimental this was to me, or that this may not even have been what he wanted. It would be many years later, when our relationship had broken, that I realized the impact this had on our marriage.

Wedding Bells

It was our eighteen-month dating anniversary and we were having a romantic dinner at a fancy restaurant when Jason insisted we drive out to a national park to look at the stars. He was not the strong romantic type, but I appreciated the effort that night. At the top of a hill, he pulled over to a lookout. We sat on the hood of the car stargazing for a few minutes, before he handed me a card. It was a dark, moonless night, and I had to turn away from him to be able to read the words with the help of the car headlights. He had penned beautiful words professing his love for me.

'There's just one more thing I need to know.'

I flipped the card over, but there were no other words. My chest tightened and I turned around to see him kneeling with a ring box opened to me.

'Will you marry me?'

For a moment, I couldn't breathe. His face was shadowed from the car lights behind him, and I couldn't see his eyes. My mind was racing. Caught in the bright headlights, I didn't know what to do. I slowly nodded *yes*.

He put the ring on my finger, scooped me up and kissed me. As he lowered me down, the ring fell off onto the gravel. I picked it up, put it back on and kept my hand in a fist until we could get it resized.

Whenever he would tell the story of his proposal, he'd say that it took a few minutes for me to nod yes because he'd caught me by surprise. I never corrected him. The truth was that in that moment our entire relationship had flashed through my mind. We were young, and he was the only long-term boyfriend I'd ever had. We were still living separate lives. We were lucky to have one or two weeknights together. We actually didn't know each other that well. We rarely talked about anything deep or meaningful. Most of our time together was spent with our families, and when we were home together, we watched TV. We didn't go out on dates because he worked most weekends and evenings and I had to be up early on weekdays. I didn't feel like I could openly talk about my thoughts and feelings because we had such contrasting world views, having been raised differently. I only showed him the parts of me I thought he wanted to see. He preferred my submissiveness, and so I made myself small and quiet. I gave in to his every desire. I agreed with him on everything. I stopped having my own opinions. We got into a pattern where, when I'd upset him, he would ignore me for days, and then I would beg for his forgiveness. When at last he showed his love, it felt like sunlight had returned, and I basked in it. I did everything to avoid the dark, silent days and keep the peace between us.

But this version of me was not all Jason's doing. In all areas of my life, I had molded myself to fit whatever persona was expected of me. I wanted to please, be loved and seen. I wanted to be special. I thought the only way was to belong to someone else, to be one half of a couple.

In that moment when he proposed, I wasn't sure I was ready to be his—or anyone's—wife. But how could I say no to marrying the person I was already living with? I didn't know how to express the truth, which was, 'I'm not sure I want to spend the rest of my life with you.' We had invested money, time and love in this relationship, but was that enough? I wasn't convinced that we were compatible for the long run. But there he was, down on one knee, absolutely certain that I belonged with him forever.

So, I said yes.

But I should have taken the ring falling from my hand as a sign.

• • •

Instead, we built a house and got married in the same year. Plans were in motion, and I tried to get excited, ignoring the nagging feeling inside. In recent times, I've spoken to many women who, like me, have ignored their intuition about this crucial life decision. Many of us are afraid of disappointing our families by calling off a wedding we know we shouldn't go through with. We are more concerned about the waste of time and money spent on planning an event than on ruining the rest of our lives. Why are we nervous about what might have happened if we turned down a proposal that wasn't right for us? Why do we feel pressured to live up to the lifelong expectation of one day being someone's wife?

Even with all these misgivings and hesitations bouncing around in my mind, I did not once seriously consider putting on the brakes or even voicing any of these concerns out loud.

The morning of the wedding, after the photographer had left, I sat on the front steps of my parents' house in my princess gown. I could hear the chatter of the bridal party from the open window. My brother came to sit next to me.

'Are you sure you want to marry him?'

I looked up at the sky, and whispered, 'It's too late to change my mind now.'

He nodded slowly. While we had never really been close or talked about our relationships, he recognized, as I did, that I was about to make a mistake.

Jason and I were married on a beautiful September day, and I have the stunning photos to prove it. The setting is picturesque, my gown is perfect, everyone is smiling. Looking at the photos now, I can see that I look stiff, without a smile in my eyes. In my memory, the wedding dinner and reception are a blur of handshaking, cheek-kissing, too many toasts and dancing. As the night came to an end and the last of the guests left, I looked for my new husband. Someone told me he had just left to drive his mom and sister back to their house. I sat on the dance floor yawning until an uncle offered to drive me home. I found my purse and texted Jason to let him know I was going home.

Once in the house, I lay on the bed waiting for him and fell asleep. Had I not been in a wedding gown, it would have been just another Saturday night.

Blue-eyed Boy

'Nine weeks, you say?' the doctor asked. I nodded, eyes filled with tears.

'Okay, lie back and lift up your shirt.'

The doctor squirted jelly on my lower belly and placed what looked like a microphone on it. He moved it around slowly. 'At nine weeks, we should be able to hear a heartbeat.'

I closed my eyes and silently begged my unborn child to stay with me. We'd agreed not to learn the gender, but I knew in my soul it was a boy.

Koosh-koosh, koosh-koosh, koosh-koosh.

I opened my eyes and looked at the doctor. He smiled. 'There it is, pretty strong for nine weeks.'

'What about the bleeding?'

'I wouldn't worry, some women bleed during the first trimester. As long as you're not having cramps or pain, you should be fine.'

While pregnant with Aidan, I took full advantage of the whole 'eating for two' thing and gave in to all of my cravings. Jason rubbed Bio-Oil on my growing belly and talked to the baby regularly. I stopped working a week before he was due, imagining that, like tracked parcels, babies arrived when they are scheduled to.

Six days after my due date, heavily pregnant and completely over it, I picked Jason up from work. In the car, he brought my hand up to his lips and kissed it.

'How are you feeling, gorgeous?'

'Heavy. And hot,' I said, rubbing my belly. I was wearing my favorite overalls, even though I couldn't do up the side buttons anymore. 'Can we stop by the store? We need some veggies.'

We drove in silence and he stroked my hand with this thumb. Standing in the produce aisle at the store, I felt a gush of warmth between my legs and looked down.

'I think my water just broke,' I whispered, mortified.

I waddled to the bathroom, squeezing for dear life, praying I wasn't leaving a wet trail behind me. I put a giant wad of paper towels in my underwear and walked back to Jason, who was still focused on the lettuce.

'We need to get to the hospital. Now,' I said in a hushed tone.

A few hours after we checked in to the maternity ward, the doctor stopped by to see how my labor was progressing. He asked about my contractions. I asked about the possibility of a meal. The nurse came in laughing. 'I hear you're hungry. I can offer you a ham and cheese sandwich if you like.'

A few hours later, we moved to the delivery room. The doctor asked if I wanted an epidural and I told him that it wasn't part of my birthing plan. The agony I felt as the hours went by also hadn't been part of my birthing plan.

'Jason,' I moaned, 'I want an epidural.'

He stroked my hair gently. 'It's okay, sweetie, just breathe. Like we learned in class.' I grabbed the collar of his shirt and pulled him an inch from my face. This pain was like nothing I'd ever experienced in my life, and I wanted it to stop.

'Get. The Fucking. Nurse.' I paused, gritting my teeth through a contraction. 'And then, go sit over there,' I continued, pointing to the chair in the corner of the room with my free hand.

One epidural and sixteen hours of labor later, the doctor placed a big baby boy on my chest. I was sweaty, sore, tired and blissful all at once. Jason kissed my forehead and told me he loved me. I looked down at this little human with big blue eyes and a full head of jet-black hair. Pure perfection.

From that moment, Aidan became my everything. He made my life brighter. He only ever cried when he needed to be fed or changed. I was mesmerized by this little boy I had brought into the world. I'd hold him long after his feeding and watch his little eyelids flutter while he slept, just as I had done as a child with baby Eva, primed for this moment. My heart was full. He was such an easy baby that I had no problems keeping up with laundry, housework and meal preparations.

He was born in late spring, and I was able to have him in the stroller outside while I did yard work. Summer flew by, and once fall rolled around, I found myself getting antsy. As much as I loved having this time with my baby boy, I was also incredibly lonely. We had only one car, which Jason drove to work most days. We were living in a new housing development and I didn't know anyone. Once in a while, I'd keep the car for outings, but because Jason still worked mid-afternoon/evening shifts, I'd have to drive him to and from work, which was exhausting. I hated having to take Aidan out of his crib at 10:30 p.m. and get him bundled into the car seat to drive the twenty minutes to Jason's office building. We ran all our errands together on weekends, which meant that I hardly ever had alone-time. A task as simple as going to the grocery store by myself to buy milk felt like heaven. I'd chat to the cashier, eager for adult interaction. I'd sit in the car in the parking lot and close my eyes. I would enjoy these quiet moments of not having to give anyone any of my time or energy.

•••

The disconnection between me and Jason that had crept in during my maternity leave started to widen. From early on, we disagreed on parenting styles. He thought I was too indulgent, and I found him too strict. I loved doting on Aidan and never minded when he wanted to be picked up and carried around. I'd let him fall asleep in my arms before carrying him to his crib to tuck him in. When he began to eat solids, we realized that he was a picky eater. I wanted to make sure he ate enough—so what if he wasn't eating the recommended fruit and vegetable servings with each meal? Jason argued that my coddling was keeping Aidan from becoming more independent. It bothered him that Aidan was so deeply attached to me. He insisted we make him eat the dreaded fruits and veggies, even if it meant he refused to eat altogether and went to bed hungry. We didn't seem to agree on anything when it came to raising our son.

Weekends were particularly stressful because he would constantly challenge the weekday routine I had put in place. We butted heads even more once I returned to work. While we were waiting for an opening in the daycare, Jason's mom offered to babysit him for us. Aidan loved spending time with her, and she would often invite me to stay for dinner when I'd pick him up after work. I appreciated these invitations—without them, between all the demands of work and home, I felt like I was drowning. I crammed the laundry, housework and meal prep into evenings and weekends, only to come home to dirty dishes on the stovetop or next to the sink. Yesterday's work clothes were dropped on the floor by the sofa, where Jason had fallen asleep watching TV after his shift. I would trip over shoes every time I walked into the house. Our bed was never made. I was exhausted most evenings when I'd get home from work, and seeing the house in such disarray made me feel like a failure as a mother and a wife.

Jason would laugh and say that he 'made the mess' and I 'cleaned it up.' Slowly, I grew to resent the fact that he didn't help me with housework and that the primary caregiving fell entirely on my shoulders.

When I felt overwhelmed, I'd look into my little boy's big blue eyes and tell myself none of this mattered, because all I saw and felt was love. As tired and frustrated as I was, I still delighted in my precious alone-time with my baby boy on weeknights. Our routine was uncomplicated and, aside from his resistance at mealtimes, he was pure joy to be around. He never ran out of hugs and kisses and his giggles made my heart burst. However, on weekends when our routine was disrupted and a new set of rules imposed, our baby had tantrums. I dreaded weekends if we didn't have plans with our extended families. It was never relaxing to spend time at home. I would get anxious, anticipating disquiet and opposition. Bedtimes became a struggle because Aidan would want to fall asleep with me, as he did most weeknights, but Jason would insist that he fall asleep on his own in his crib. The sounds of his cries tugged at my heart, and as much as I wanted to comfort him, I couldn't face the angry words followed by cold silences from my husband.

I often found myself fantasizing about a life where it was just me and my son.

Unexpected Gift

We leaned on the counter, staring at the little window on the test. My co-worker had convinced me to get a pregnancy test from the pharmacy.

'It's better to know. I'll stay with you,' she'd said.

I was on birth control and hardly ever had sex with Jason. But my period was late and my pants were snug.

Two pink lines.

'Maybe this'll be a good thing for you guys,' she said. 'It could help you reconnect?'

I nodded. 'Maybe.'

Jason and I had grown accustomed to crossing paths only on weekends. Most nights, after work, he'd fall asleep on the sofa. In earlier years, I'd wake him so he would come to bed with me. I stopped when I realized I preferred sleeping alone. I didn't have to worry about being woken up when he'd move me so he could cuddle up, which was his preferred way of sleeping. I also didn't have to fret about him getting upset if Aidan was sleeping with me.

I'd almost always give in to my boy and let him crawl into bed with me, because it was the only way to get a decent sleep.

I brought the pregnancy test home and left it where I knew Jason would see it.

'Are you sure?' he asked after getting back from work.

I was already in bed.

'Yep.'

He lay down next to me, his face close to mine. 'This is good,' he whispered.

I nodded and rolled over to face the wall.

Our relationship was already so strained. How could a baby save us? We hadn't wanted to know the gender when I was pregnant with Aidan, but this time, I insisted we find out. Jason resisted, but when I asked the technician at the sonogram he didn't argue.

'You're having a girl,' she'd said with a big grin. My heart fluttered. *My own little baby girl.* I was thrilled.

I worked as long as I could so that the majority of my leave would be after her birth. This pregnancy was very different from my first, and the months flew by. It was a busy period at work and I didn't always find the time to eat. Between not taking the best care of myself and chasing a toddler, I hardly gained any weight. I was always tired and had terrible mood swings. Aidan was so excited about having a baby sister to play with. He would kiss my belly and talk to it. He'd place his stuffed animals on my growing bump when I read him bedtime stories.

'Look, Mommy, I share with the baby.'

He'd pour water on my tummy with plastic toys when we took baths together.

'I wash the baby,' he'd say, giggling. I was finally able to get him to stay in his big-boy bed about a month before she was born. And although Jason and I still weren't in a great place, we were making the effort to be kinder to each other. I suppose we both hoped this little miracle might be the bridge linking us back to one another.

I was sitting in the hospital waiting room a week past my due date, leafing through a glossy magazine about the summer style trends, when I heard the nurse call my name. I felt another contraction coming on and looked at my phone. Only eight minutes since the last one. I was surely going to meet my baby girl today. When Jason had left the house earlier that morning, I'd reminded him about my checkup and asked that he leave his cellphone on.

'You know I can't have the ringer on at work, Sonia.' He'd kissed my cheek, ruffled Aidan's hair and left for the workday.

The doctor walked in. I was lying on the examination table, feet in stirrups. 'My labor started at around 4 a.m. and my contractions are about seven to eight minutes apart,' I informed him casually.

He laughed. 'I don't think you'd be this calm if you were in labor.'

I persuaded him to send me up to the maternity ward for observation. Less than thirty minutes later, I was in a hospital gown, standing at a payphone. The nursing staff suggested I get ahold of my husband quickly, because this baby seemed eager to meet us. I called Jason's cellphone and it went straight to voicemail. I slammed the receiver. Left with no choice, I called the general help line for the call center where he worked. 'Canada Revenue Agency Helpline, Andrew speaking, may I please have your Social Insurance Number or Tax Identification Number?'

'Hi, Andrew. I'm hoping you can help me. I'm Jason's wife; he works at the call center with you.' I paused. 'Could you please let him know that I'm in labor and that he really needs to get to the hospital?'

Silence. 'Okay. Yes, uh, yes. Jason, right. I'll, uh, I'll let him know that you're having the baby.' I hung up laughing, knowing that all calls were recorded and used for training purposes.

The contractions were only a few minutes apart, and Jason still hadn't arrived. I pressed the button to call for the nurse. I asked for an epidural but it was too late. I was fully dilated and it was time to push, just as I heard Jason's voice in the hallway. The nurse brought him in. He kissed my forehead and held my hand. I pushed as hard as I could, remembering how long and painful this part had been with Aidan. After two more pushes, my baby came out into the world and uttered a small cry. The doctor cut the umbilical cord and placed her on my chest. She was much lighter than Aidan had been at birth, and I sat up to get a better look at her. She scrunched her little nose and stuck out her tongue. She opened her eyes and stared at me with a stern, unimpressed gaze. I laughed when the nurse said that she seemed peeved to be out of the womb. I breathed her in as I kissed the top of her little head.

Cassie Jeanine was born on a Friday afternoon, and by Sunday morning, we were back at home. We were still on the waiting list for Aidan to attend daycare when Jason returned to work the next day. I had hoped that Jason's mom might offer to take him a few hours a day while I adjusted to having a two-year-old and a newborn, but I was too proud to ask for help. I suppose I wanted to prove that I could do it all on my own. I had spent my childhood around babies and young children, and I didn't want to be perceived as incapable of mothering my own kids by asking for support. I didn't realize that I was in over my head. I told myself to just do what I was supposed to and be a perfect mother.

Instead of reaching out for someone to throw me a buoy, I continued treading water. Until I nearly drowned.

All the time spent around kids in my childhood did not prepare me for the shock of going from one child to two. Cassie cried relentlessly for the first nine months of her life. She would only calm down if I cradled her in the crook of my arm—not in the sling that might allow me to get some chores done. She had to be tucked in between my body and my arm. I became adept at doing laundry, vacuuming, cleaning, and cooking with one hand. I also had a toddler who was very attached to me and didn't appreciate no longer having my undivided attention. I was ragged with exhaustion.

Jason tried to help but would get frustrated with all the whining and crying. 'They want you, not me,' he'd say, irritated. I'd get angry that he wasn't trying harder to engage with Aidan, or connect with Cassie. I'd beg him to change his work shifts so that he could be around more.

I had insisted we buy a second car once Cassie was born. I was terrified of the isolation and loneliness I had felt during my first maternity leave. I wanted to be able to take the kids to visit their grandparents and go out whenever I wanted. Even with this physical freedom, I still struggled. I was sinking, desperately trying to stay afloat in the sea of soiled diapers, feedings, laundry, potty training and sleeplessness. I never seemed to be able to get on top of things. Far from believing I'd been primed to be a great mother from when I was a toddler, more and more I felt like a complete failure.

Depression slowly started to seep in, although I didn't know it at the time. I was closing in on myself. I felt sluggish, as my daily life became heavy and suffocating. I went through the motions of what I was meant to do, but without any emotion. I began to have frightening thoughts about ending the pain I felt, but I didn't talk to anyone about them. These played through my mind like a movie reel. I didn't want to continue living like this. In all honesty, I didn't want to continue living at all. I believed in my bones that my husband and kids would be better off without me. I imagined getting in the car, driving off and never coming back. Driving across the bridge that connected my parents' town to mine, I'd sometimes imagine myself swerving into the lake and drowning for real. I'd stand in our bathroom and take out all the pain medicine we had. I'd have to bite my hand to stop myself from swallowing them all down. I wanted the immense heaviness of my pain to dissipate, and I thought the only way it would was if I died. I don't know what stopped me. I believe it was divine intervention, a small whisper that nudged me away from these dark thoughts.

While I'd read about the 'baby blues' in my prenatal books, this felt heavier than just *the blues*. I was embarrassed and ashamed that I could not connect with my newborn baby. I felt like a fraud as a wife and a mother. I didn't know who to turn to or even how to articulate what I was feeling. I was scared of what I might do to myself, or worse, to my children. And in this state, I was paralyzed. I knew I needed to ask for help, but I didn't know who to turn to. I had always been a pleaser, a good girl who followed the rules and did all the right things. Why was this happening?

Now, looking back at that dark episode of my life, I believe my baby girl came to me because my soul needed her. Her birth was a catalyst for my emotional and physical breakdown. The way she came crashing into my world broke me. I needed that. Among all the literature I have since devoured about depression, I once read that depression is your soul's way of forcing you into 'deep rest.' It pushes you to deconstruct the world that you've created around yourself, out of fear and a need for safety. To look at the shadow parts of your being that you've been running from and make peace with them. Depression makes everything dark, allowing you to find your light.

My postpartum depression forced me to look at the life I had created and the choices I had made in order to please those around me. I could no longer ignore how I had changed myself to the core to avoid conflicts.

When Aidan was born, I knew what I was doing. I was comfortable holding him, carrying him, feeding him, changing him. I was more connected to him than I had ever been to any other person in my life. I sensed his needs before he even uttered a small yelp. This dynamic completely changed once Cassie was born. Now I had my hands full. And, somehow, I forgot everything I knew about babies and children.

I had spent most of my life around kids of all ages. I had helped feed the smaller ones. I'd gone around the table with a facecloth, cleaning dirty faces. I'd changed diapers, warmed up bottles, wiped bums, handed out snacks. I always had a small child sitting in my lap. I'd read to them, brush their hair, help wash their hands after using the toilet. I was patient and rarely lost my temper or became annoyed. I had been born for motherhood—at least, that was the narrative I'd inherited about myself. Suddenly, it was as though everything that had been ingrained in me from a young age had been surgically removed. I felt awkward and unnatural. I didn't intuitively know what my own baby girl wanted or needed, and she would cry and cry and cry until I could find a way to soothe her. Nothing ever worked twice to calm her. Aidan became increasingly demanding, not wanting to share his beloved mommy with the crying baby.

•••

Nights were the worst. It was a little after 2 a.m. on one of those nights. I had been in a fog all day and was so tired I couldn't see clearly. I heard her slight whimper and jumped out of bed. I had to get to her before it turned into a full-blown cry and she'd wake her brother up. He'd only just started sleeping through the night, and I really needed him to keep it up.

I walked in and turned on the glowing moon light above her crib. She looked up and stopped fussing as I put the pacifier in her mouth. I stared at her for a minute, waiting to feel something. I picked her up, gently laid her on the change table and unsnapped her onesie. I took off her soiled diaper, cleaned her and put on a dry one. I looked at her again briefly as I snapped up the onesie, trying to avoid her gaze. I swear she knew. I picked her up, walked into the kitchen and turned on the oven light. I ran the hot water tap and took the bottle out of the fridge.

She was growing impatient and began to wriggle in my arms. She spat out the pacifier and started to cry. 'I should just microwave these damn things,' I thought, swaying from side to side, holding the pacifier in her mouth with my chin to stop her from crying.

It was finally warm enough. I turned the tap off, started walking and caught my hip on the corner of the counter. 'Fucking hell,' I muttered. I looked at the dining room table with the mounting pile of clean laundry and told myself I'd deal with it tomorrow. Or maybe, if I left it long enough, Jason might fold it and put it away. I sat on the sofa and started to feed her. She sucked greedily at her bottle, staring at me. I heard a slight thump and closed my eyes.

'God, no, please, not again tonight.' I took a deep breath and when I opened my eyes, Aidan was standing in front of me, still half-asleep.

'Mommy, I can't sleep. Come to my bed with me.'

'Aidan, honey, Mommy is feeding the baby. I need you to go back to bed, okay? Mommy will come in as soon as Cassie's done her bottle to tuck you in.' I tried to keep my voice quiet.

'No, Mommy. Come now,' he said, stomping his foot. He was pouting, his eyes defiant. I sensed we were about one minute away from a full-blown tantrum. *Maybe I should just let him scream and shout. Maybe then, Jason would wake up and help me.* He took a step closer and reached out for me.

I closed my eyes and rubbed my forehead. Taking a deep breath, I looked at him. I gently rubbed his little belly and said, 'Aidan, Mommy will be in very soon, I promise, okay? Now, please, be my good boy and go back to bed.' He frowned, his mouth tightening.

I felt Cassie push the bottle out of her mouth. When I looked down, I saw formula was dripping down her neck. I sat her up to burp her. Aidan stood, pulling down at the front waistband of his Spiderman pajamas, his lower lip quivering, eyes tearing up.

'Mommyyyy …' he whined. I looked at him and everything slowed down. His crying sounds were muffled, and I couldn't see clearly. The fog closed in on me. I talked myself down, reminding myself not to yell or shake him, not to grab him by the arm and drag him back to his bedroom kicking and screaming. I blinked and everything came back into focus. I stood with the baby cradled in my arm, holding the bottle in her mouth with my chin. I took Aidan's hand and walked him back to his room. I told myself that he was just a small child; he didn't know any better. His world had been turned upside-down with the arrival of his baby sister, and he also probably sensed me slowly disappearing.

He climbed into his bed, and I sat next to him as I fed her, the moon light still glowing in her room. He was back asleep in minutes and she finished her bottle. I carefully pulled the covers over his shoulders. My boy, my sweet, sweet boy. I remembered how it was not very long ago, when my heart would swell when he looked at me and how his laughter brought me so much joy. There was a time when I couldn't get enough of him. But in that moment, standing, watching him sleeping peacefully, I felt nothing.

I walked across the hall and laid my baby in the crib. I pulled the blanket up to her belly and put the pacifier in her mouth. I looked at her in the glow of the moon light and could see why everyone told me how pretty she was, with her soft brown hair, rosy cheeks and long lashes. I shook my head, turned the light off and walked back to the kitchen. I rinsed the bottle, turned the oven light off and found my way back to my bed.

I lay there for a minute, looking at Jason in the glow of the streetlight and wondered how he could sleep through all that crying, night after night. How could he not see that I was drowning?

•••

The next morning, I decided to call the only person I knew who might be able to help me—Eva. If I could open up to anyone about what was happening, it was her. She and I shared a lifelong bond that began when she was a baby and I'd stroke her forehead to help her fall back asleep at my mother's daycare, to the times when we started having babies of our own. I needed to talk to someone who might understand what I was feeling. I sat on the front steps of the house, leaving both kids inside. My hands were shaking as I listened to the ringtone, praying for her to answer. After the usual pleasantries, I asked her, 'Remember when you had Alex? How you felt really down?'

'I do. What's going on with you? Is everything okay?'

'It's weird, but I can see how some women drown their kids in the tub or, like, smother them with pillows in their sleep.'

I heard her take a sharp breath. 'Are you thinking about doing this? You need to be real with me here.'

'Sometimes,' I whispered. 'Some days, when she won't stop crying or, at night, when Aidan gets up and they both cry and cry, I just, I just want it to stop. I am so fucking tired.'

'Isn't Jason helping you? He could get up with Cassie and feed her, no?'

'Yeah, in a perfect world,' I snickered. 'Aidan got up again last night and I swear to God, it took everything within me not to smack him or shake him. I wanted to drag him back to his bedroom by the arm, throw him in his bed and …'

'And what? Did you?'

'No. I didn't. But I'm worried that I might do something.' I looked across the street at some kids playing in the park. 'Sometimes, when I'm driving across the bridge, I wonder what would happen if I swerved into the lake.' I felt the hot tears start to pool in my eyes.

'Shit, Sonia, that's not good. Look, I had a hard time after Alex was born. Like, a really hard time, but I got help and I got some rest and took some meds, and everything that I did got me through it. I'm worried about you. I think you need a break.'

I wiped my cheeks and nose with the back of my hand and exhaled loudly. 'Oh wow. I didn't mean to worry you. I just needed to vent. I promise you that I will not actually drive off a bridge,' I said, trying to sound light. 'Anyway, the kids are crying again. Gotta go. Love you.' I hung up and sat a while longer.

I wondered if Eva was right to worry that I might actually do something terrible if I didn't get the help I desperately needed.

Family Secrets

Throughout my childhood, I witnessed my grandmother suffer from deep bouts of what I now know to be depression. She was often withdrawn, moody, and seemed confused. She rarely smiled, and I don't think I ever heard her laugh. We never knew which version of her would open the door to greet us, and I didn't feel safe around her, preferring to stick close to my mom.

    I knew she had battled breast cancer before I was born and thought that perhaps the anguish of the disease had hardened her. Most of my memories of her center around the holiday season. We would always go to her apartment for lunch on Christmas day. It wasn't uncommon for her to suddenly stand up from the kitchen table where we were all enjoying a meal, throw her plate of food in the sink and lock herself in her bedroom. My mom, sister and I would clean up after we were done eating, while my dad, uncle and brother watched sports on TV. She would either rejoin us a while later, acting as though this behavior was completely normal, or my dad would knock on the door and try to convince her to come out. If she didn't, my mom would prepare a dinner plate for my uncle and we would leave. Whenever I'd ask what was wrong with her, my parents would say that she was having an 'episode.' I didn't know that meant, but my young mind was satisfied with this answer.

My grandparents separated later in life, and my grandmother moved to the city with her adult son. My uncle had cerebral palsy and lived with her until she became sick again. I was fairly young during a particularly bad episode when she had to be admitted to the psychiatric ward. The apartment building manager called my dad to let him know that they had sent her to the hospital via ambulance and that my uncle couldn't stay in the apartment alone because of his mobility issues. My uncle moved in with us for a couple of weeks while she was in the hospital. These were trying times for my dad. He's from a generation of tough love, raised by heavy drinkers, and was often left to care for his handicapped brother. I never heard him speak ill of his parents, childhood or upbringing. He's not the type of person to complain about what life has put him through. But growing up in this environment must have taken a toll on him as a young boy and teenager. Perhaps this explains why I rarely witnessed his sensitive side when I was a child. Not understanding depression, maybe he saw my grandmother's inability to cope with the world around her as a weakness. In his eyes, being unable to escape sorrow and showing vulnerability and fragility were flaws. He loved us deeply but always maintained a tough-guy attitude.

I remember visiting my grandmother in the psychiatric ward. I looked at the people sitting at round tables in this big, bright room with bars on the windows. Most people were in their pajamas or wearing hospital gowns with robes. There was a peculiar smell in the room, like bad breath and poor hygiene, mixed with chemical disinfectant. A few people were watching TV, including a man in a rocking chair wearing a padded helmet. My mom saw me staring at him while he rocked back and forth, his head hitting the back of the chair repeatedly. She squeezed my hand, whispering that it was rude to stare at people.

Grandma's speech was slurred, and she asked the same questions over and over again. Mom explained that the medication she took made her tired.

Part way through our visit, a tall woman walked over to our table and started petting my head with her hands. She stood there, humming and running her fingers through my hair. I froze, terrified, and my mom told my dad we would wait in the car for him. She took my hand and walked me out of the room. We had to get one of the nurses to let us out of the ward.

After this visit, I became increasingly uneasy around my grandma. I wondered if her episodes were contagious, like a cold. I was terrified at the thought of ever having to stay in a facility like the one she was in.

Now that I've been through depression, I see that the stigma surrounding mental disease is undeserved. People suffering from anxiety, depression and other forms of mental illness are often misunderstood. No one chooses to be depressed. I never wanted to feel stuck in a darkness that threatened to drown me at any given moment. I would have loved nothing more than to look at my newborn baby girl and marvel at her pure perfection. I wanted my heart to burst with so much love and joy. But that didn't happen. Instead, I was thrust into the hardest moments of my life. Fortunately, this happened to me in an era where mental illness was addressed in a healthier way.

While not everyone around me understood what I was going through, I was able to access the support I needed through my doctor, parents and a few close friends. They did not judge me or make me feel worse than I already did; they rallied around me and asked how they could help. They allowed me the time and space I needed to find the different healing modalities that brought me back to myself, which I continue to use to this day to help me live with anxiety and depression.

My illness is no different from diabetes or heart disease, in that it simply requires proper treatment, without stigmatization. I try to be as honest and open as I can about what I've been through and continue to live with. It's important to me that I not only showcase the good parts of my life but also acknowledge my struggles and continue to ask for help when I need it.

My hope is that by modelling this behavior, I've laid the groundwork for my children to reach out for support if either ever find themselves in a dark place.

Down Came The Rain

I was still sitting on the front steps of the house when my phone rang. It was a warm summer day and the sky was perfectly clear. I could hear both kids crying through the open window. I tried to shut the sound out. 'Hello?'

'Hi, Sonia, it's Mom. How are you?'

'I'm good,' I said in a flat tone.

'How are the kids?' Silence.

Alive, I thought.

'Is that Aidan I hear crying?' she continued.

I looked up at him, standing at the window.

'Is he okay?' she asked, sounding concerned.

'He's crying because he wants me to hold him,' I said, looking at a couple in the distance walking towards the house.

'Where are the kids right now?'

'In the house. Cassie's in her crib. She won't stop crying.'

I heard what sounded like a hand on the receiver and whispering in a hushed tone.

'I'm just sitting on the front steps,' I continued.

The couple was getting closer now. I looked at them. 'There's some people walking by; maybe they'll want to take the kids for a while. I should ask them. They look like nice people.'

'Sonia,' she shouted, which snapped me out of my haze. 'Listen to me. Dad is on his way. He's going to pick you guys up. You're going to come and stay with us for a few days, okay? We'll help you with the kids, and you can get some rest.'

The couple walked past and smiled at me. The lady looked up at the crying toddler in the window. She turned back and gave me a soft, knowing look.

'Sonia? Are you there?'

'I'm here.' I sighed. 'I'll go in and pack a bag.' I heard her snapping her fingers.

'Dad's on his way. It'll be okay.' I looked up at the window. Aidan was staring at me, pulling on his waistband, his eyes red and puffy. I walked into the house and picked him up, and we sat on the sofa together, while Cassie cried in her crib.

A few hours later, we were in the car with my dad. I'd told Jason that my parents offered to have me and the kids stay with them for a few days so I could get some rest. He agreed that it was a good idea. Maybe he could see that I was not doing great after all.

On the way to my parents' house, we pulled into the clinic I used to go to as a child. 'Why are we stopping here?'

'Your mom called the doctor and he wants to see you.'

I felt ambushed. 'Dad, I can't go to him. He's not covered by my insurance.'

'Let's not worry about that right now. I'll get Aidan out of his car seat; you just take Cassie and go in. They are waiting for you,' he said.

'Mommy, no, don't go.' Aidan's lower lip started quivering.

I put Cassie's car seat on the ground beside the car. 'It's okay, Dad, I'll take him.' Aidan wiped his damp eyes. Tantrum averted. The receptionist at the front desk recognized me and ushered me into one of the exam rooms. I put the car seat on the floor. Cassie was still sleeping from the car ride. I sat Aidan on the examination bed next to me. He moved into my lap, facing me, and wrapped his arms around my neck.

The doctor walked in with a sympathetic smile. Sitting on the small stool, he turned to me.

'Sonia, it's been a while since I've seen you. How are you feeling?'

How was I feeling? That was a loaded question. I looked up at the clock on the wall, biting the inside of my lower lip. 'Not so good.' My whole body started shaking and I put Aidan on the floor. He didn't fight me. The doctor opened the door and whispered something to a nurse, who came in with a lollipop. She led Aidan out to my dad in the waiting room.

The doctor placed a box of tissues next to me. I was crying so hard I couldn't see. I wiped my nose on my sleeve.

'I'm tired. I'm so tired, and I'm scared that I might do something bad.' I told him about the previous night, how I was worried I might hurt myself or my kids. I told him all of the bad thoughts that had been going through my head for the last few weeks. I told him that I felt lost in a fog. That I couldn't seem to find my way out of it.

He asked me about the birth, about the baby, was she a good baby, did she eat well, did she sleep, did I have any support at home, was I eating, was I sleeping, was Aidan in daycare or was he home with me, and the list went on.

I answered all his questions openly. He explained that while it's very normal to have a period where you feel sad or blue after giving birth, for some women, it can be worse; that I was not losing my mind. There was a medical term for what I was experiencing—postpartum depression.

'I think it would be prudent for you to start taking antidepressants to help rebalance your hormones. They will take some time to start working.' He paused. 'But they will help you to feel better. As opposed to the way you do now.'

I nodded. 'Okay.'

I was grateful to Eva for listening to me, hearing my cry for help and reaching out to my parents. We'd had our kids staggered over four years. Aidan was almost a year old when she had her first son. I remember visiting her and noticing her exhaustion, that the light in her eyes had dimmed.

She'd opened up to me about how much she was struggling, but I hadn't really listened; I wasn't sympathetic. I had minimized her fears and feelings, telling her that it was just the baby blues. I'd left her alone in this state. I still feel ashamed when I think back to that day. I didn't want to see or hear what she was feeling, and I brushed over what she was going through. I couldn't understand because, when I had my son, I felt nothing but pure joy. I will never be able to apologize enough for my indifference and ignorance.

All I can do now is be open and honest about my own experiences with postpartum depression. I refuse to attach any shame to what I went through. Women are expected to bask in the blissfulness of motherhood—yet another achievement that completes us. And for some, I believe this to be true. But for others, it's a much darker road. Without support, it's easy to get lost.

Luckily, I was able to get the help that I needed.

A Mother's Love

I stayed at my parents' house for two weeks. With each day that passed, each healthy meal I ate, each hour of sleep I got, I started to feel the darkness subside. I took my antidepressants every morning like clockwork, and Aidan quickly noticed.

'Mommy, what's that?' he asked one morning as I took the pill my mom handed me.

'It's Mommy's special vitamin, kiddo. To help me feel better,' I said, smiling at him.

My mom opened a cupboard and handed him a vitamin gummy. I had forgotten that she kept those for the kids at the daycare.

'Here you go, Aidan, now you have your own vitamins. Don't ever touch Mommy's, okay?'

'Okay, Mami,' he said with a big grin.

Cassie cried in the playpen. I started to stand up, but my dad placed his hand on my shoulder as he walked by. 'I've got her.'

He bent over the playpen cooing and slowly picked her up. He put his face near her tummy. 'Pheewwww, you stink, little girl.' He disappeared into the other room. She was making slight noises while he whispered to her and changed her diaper. My dad had taken six weeks off work after our births to help my mom recover. He believed that she had done the hard part by growing and birthing us and that she deserved a rest. He took care of the bulk of feedings, diaper changes and bath times. He loved this bonding time, being witness to all the changes that took place in those first six weeks. Now I watched as he laid Cassie on a blanket on the dining room table in front of me and put his hand on my shoulder. 'She looks exactly like you, you know.'

She stared at me, her little feet kicking. I looked into her eyes; they were still hazel, like Jason's. Little flecks of gold reflected back when she looked up at the light. She started fussing, and my dad reached for her.

'It's okay, I'll take her,' I said.

My mom, always one step ahead, was already warming up a bottle under the hot water tap. Getting impatient, Cassie pulled at my nightgown with her uncoordinated little hands. I sat on the sofa and placed a pillow on my lap. I laid her down, rubbing the tip of the bottle on her lips. She sucked on it urgently and then slowed down. As she drank, I traced from the bridge of her nose to her forehead with my finger.

I was reminded of the times I kneeled by this very sofa, watching Eva sleep. How patient I had been, even as a small child, looking over the baby girl. Why couldn't I feel the same love and wonder for my own baby? Why couldn't I connect with her? Maybe the pills would fix me. Maybe having support and getting some sleep would help. I held on to that tiny bit of hope.

She was looking deeply into my eyes, and I felt a slight stir. When I finished feeding her, I handed her to my dad, who was already sitting in the rocking chair, waiting. He'd spend hours rocking her, cradled in his arms. I looked at them and smiled, wondering if this reminded him of when I was a baby.

'Mind if I go take a shower?' I asked my mom.

'Go ahead. Take your time,' she said while sorting grapes and crackers into small bowls. She was always busy preparing the next meal or snack. Witnessing her expertly planning and preparing for the next thing only amplified my feelings of inadequacy. I'd grown up in an environment of preparing, scheduling and perfectionism, and yet I could not seem to get my shit together. I wondered if I'd ever get back to a place where I felt like I was in control.

I walked up the stairs to my childhood bedroom. Aidan and I were sharing the single bed, which he was loving. My parents had set up a second playpen for Cassie in their bedroom. They took turns getting up for her nighttime feedings. I gathered clothes and headed to the bathroom. I turned on the shower and waited for the water warm up. Taking off my nightgown, I looked at my reflection in the mirror. My belly was still swollen, my breasts engorged and tender, the veins dark beneath the stretched skin. I traced the stretch marks on my belly with my fingernails and felt tears stinging my eyes. I opened the medicine cabinet and saw my mom's heart medication, the one she'd taken most of her life.

'You can never, ever touch these pills, Sonia. If you take even just one, your heart will stop beating and you will die,' she would remind me every time I watched her take it as a child.

I opened the lid and dumped the contents of the bottle into the palm of my hand. It would be an easy way to go. My heart would simply stop and all of the pain and sorrow I was feeling would go away. My husband and kids would be better off without me. I stared at the pills, tears streaming down my cheeks. The knock at the door jolted me.

'Sonia, Aidan's crying. He couldn't see you and got worried, so I brought him up.'

I scrambled to put the pills back in the bottle and return it to where I had found it in the medicine cabinet. I wiped my nose on the back of my hand.

'Could you take his clothes off? He can just shower with me and I won't have to give him a bath tonight.'

She opened the bathroom door and nudged a naked Aidan in. 'Look who I found. Do you want to have a shower with Mommy?'

He wiped his eyes and smiled. 'Hi, Mommy, I was crying because I thought I lost you.'

We sat together in the tub, letting the water wash away our tears. I held him tight and kissed his little face. I whispered that I loved him.

He will never know all the times he saved me from myself.

It pains me that my children had to go through this depression with me. For the first nine months of her life, I couldn't connect emotionally with Cassie. I was physically around, but my heart wasn't in it. And Aidan went from having a loving, doting mother to being cared for by a shell of a human being, devoid of feelings.

He lost me time and time again, both physically and emotionally.

Happy Pills

I was daunted by the thought of returning home after those two weeks, worried I'd fall back into the abyss of darkness I was finally managing to escape. Jason had visited for a few hours on the weekends. On the drive home, I asked him what he had told his family about where I'd been.

'What do you mean? I told them that you went to stay with your parents for a while. That they wanted you to visit with the kids.'

'Did you tell them about my postpartum depression? That I'm taking meds for it?'

He looked at me, crossly. 'No. I didn't tell them anything about that. Besides, I still don't understand why you're taking those pills.' His jaw tightened. 'It's all a state of mind. Being happy is a choice.'

I looked out the window, shaking my head. I turned back to him. 'You think I want to feel like this?'

He shrugged. 'Whatever. Let's not talk about it in front of Aidan. He doesn't need to think there's something wrong with you. He's clingy enough as it is.'

'Jason, there *is* something wrong with me.' I turned and gazed out the window again, fighting back the tears. He continued to look at the road straight ahead.

As I lifted my bag from the trunk in our driveway, I stared at the house on whose front stairs I had sat just a few weeks ago, wanting to give my kids to strangers. Maybe if I opened the windows and aired it out, the darkness would leave.

We spent the evening in silence. I made dinner, gave Aidan his bath, fed and changed Cassie and put the kids to bed. I sat on the sofa next to Jason watching TV. I wondered if I should try talking to him again. Maybe if I opened up and explained what I was feeling, he'd understand. I looked at the clock: 9:30 p.m. Cassie would be up in about three hours, and then three hours after that.

'I'm going to get ready for bed,' I said.

His eyes were still glued to the screen. 'Okay. Are you going to get up when she wakes up, or do you want me to feed her?'

'Could you? I could use the extra few hours of sleep.'

He glanced over at me. 'As long as it's before midnight. I have to work tomorrow. You get to stay at home all day.' Jason presumed being home all day meant I was relaxing and lounging around. If anything, staying home with a toddler and a newborn was harder work than any job I'd ever had. Not to mention the shift is never over. I rolled my eyes as I closed the bedroom door.

Cassie's cries woke me up a few hours later. I rushed to her, hoping Aidan wouldn't wake up. I looked at Jason rocking her side to side as he tried to feed her. She was wailing and stiffening her little body against his, turning her head away from the bottle. He looked up and saw me standing in the hallway. Frustrated, he handed her over, along with the bottle.

'She won't take it from me,' he said as he stormed to the washroom. I gently swayed her from side to side until she calmed down and then sat on the sofa and gave her the bottle. I put her back in her crib when she was done and returned to bed. I looked over at Jason's shadow, his chest moving up and down rhythmically.

'Jason,' I whispered. I held my breath and waited. 'Thanks for trying.' He didn't move. I turned over and looked at the clock. With any luck, I'd get four hours of sleep before the kids woke up.

• • •

The next morning, Jason walked into the kitchen where Aidan and I were having breakfast. I handed Cassie over to him. 'She needs to be changed,' I said, filling a glass with water.

'Hello, princess,' he cooed as he kissed her face.

I opened my pill bottle and took one out. Aidan was watching me and put his hand out asking for his vitamin. I handed him a gummy one.

'Look, Daddy, I take a vitamin, too.'

Jason shook his head, smiling at Aidan and said, 'Those aren't Mommy's vitamins.' He paused and looked directly into my eyes. 'Those are her happy pills. She has to take them because we don't make her happy anymore.'

With that, he turned and walked out, with Cassie cradled in his arms. Standing at the kitchen sink, I leaned forward and dropped my head into my hands at the assault of his words.

I was shaking with rage and despair at the thought my children would think I didn't love them. Why would my husband say something so unfair in front of our son, who was just a toddler? We both knew Aidan was hyper-focused on me since Cassie's birth and would cry if I was out of his line of sight. He sensed something was different about me.

From that moment, Jason had sealed the narrative for Aidan about my antidepressants, and I decided not to take them in front of him ever again. I felt so much shame when Aidan started referring to my medication as 'Mommy's happy pills.'

It hurt me deeply to have my pain turned into some sort of a joke and to realize that my husband believed I was choosing not to be happy. I longed for him to understand that no amount of sunshine, fresh air or positive thinking could help me get better until the chemical imbalance in my brain had been corrected with the proper medication. I didn't have the energy to disagree, fight or try and make him see through my lens, and so I gave up. I decided to focus the little bit of fight I had left in me on defeating my true opponent, my depression.

I was nervous about telling his family I was suffering from postpartum depression. I knew they didn't think of mental illness as a 'real' disease. When I confided in them, I got the same advice over and over again—*go for walk outside, the sunshine will help; get some sleep, you'll feel better; be sure to nap when the baby naps.* And of course: *you just have to choose to be happy, Sonia.* Unheard, unseen and, most devastatingly, unsupported, I felt judged by the very people who were supposed to love me.

The medication didn't return me to normal, although I'm not really sure what my 'normal' self was supposed to be. I didn't feel sad anymore; the fog lifted, but I didn't feel happy. I was numb. I was emotionally flatlining, without any ups or downs. In this state of detachment, it was difficult for me to care about anyone else's needs. No one was taking care of me, except me. I knew I had to focus on myself and make sure I was getting what I needed, so I could keep going for the sake of the kids. The only way I would get through this was by putting myself first. I was the only one who could rescue me.

Over the coming months, I stopped being a doormat. If I didn't agree with something, I started speaking up. I clapped back. I refused to continue accepting behaviours that for years I had chosen to disregard. I was done being a perfect wife and mother. I was done trying to please everyone.

But even as I was becoming stronger, I felt completely alone, until I saw an interview with Brooke Shields on *Oprah* when Cassie was ten months old. She had written a book on her experience with postpartum depression. She talked about how her life, a life that she loved, suddenly felt stifling. She longed to escape the pain and sadness she felt whenever she was around her newborn daughter. She simply could not connect with her baby.

'And then we also have this image of motherhood, you know, the breastfeeding and hair cascading down and connection with the infant instantly. I did not have that. I felt like a failure as a mother,' she said, her words echoing my thoughts.

I immediately packed the kids in the car and drove straight to the nearest bookstore. Over the next few days, I devoured her memoir. Every word she wrote spoke to me and made sense of my own experience. Because of this book, I was able, for the first time, to express my thoughts, fears and feelings. I finally had a language in which to speak about the unspeakable. From then on, I handed copies of it to friends and family saying, 'This. You want to know what I'm going through and how you can help, read this.'

One night, I handed the book to Jason when he was watching TV. He glanced at the cover.

'What's this?'

'It's a book about postpartum depression by Brooke Shields. I'd like you to read it. I think it could help you understand what I'm going through.'

He dropped it on the side table and returned his attention to his show without saying a single word.

If I had to pick the exact moment when I realized my marriage was over, this was it.

The book sat on the side table for several weeks, collecting dust.

• • •

Ever since I was a child, I had been told I would be a wonderful mom. That honestly is the biggest lie I've ever been fed. Recently, someone asked me if I'd wanted to be a mother and had dreamed of one day having children of my own. The only way I know how to answer this question is that I'd always thought my life purpose was to find a man, get married and have children, because that is what I was told to imagine. I didn't question this. I didn't push against it or dream there was an alternative. I ended up being a mother, with all the pain and drama that has brought. And though my relationships with my kids are complex and different from the ones other mothers may have, I have never regretted motherhood. Through it, I have learned so much about myself—my strengths as well as my vulnerabilities and failures.

But here's where I part ways with my history and am actively challenging and changing the narrative: I want my daughter to know that she has a choice. I hope she is the first woman in our family lineage to forge her own path, by either opting for motherhood (in whatever shape feels right for her) or rejecting it for some other life path she elects.

Buster

When Cassie was eighteen months old, Jason suggested that we get a puppy.

'I grew up with a dog, and I think it'd be good for the kids. Teach them some responsibility,' he said.

Meanwhile, I was back at work, still trying to pull myself out of my depression, finally feeling like I had gained a little bit of control. The last thing I wanted or needed was to add a dog to my list of creatures to keep alive. The kids and I had gotten into a routine on weekdays when we were alone, while weekends remained a challenge. One sunny Saturday afternoon, Jason proposed that we go for a drive out to the country. The kids were due for their naps and always fell asleep quickly in the van, so I agreed. We'd been driving for forty-five minutes when he pulled into a secluded driveway and parked next to a red barn.

'Ummm, where are we?' I asked, as a woman came out of the barn.

'We're picking up our new puppy,' he responded casually.

'What? What are you talking about? I told you that I don't want a puppy,' I said in a hushed tone.

Ignoring me, he took the kids out of the car. He shook hands with the woman, and I watched them go into the barn. When I'd composed myself enough to join them, I found Aidan petting a black and white Boston terrier. 'Can we call him Buster?' he asked, beaming. I looked over at Jason, who was counting out cash.

'Sure thing, kiddo,' I said, forcing myself to remain calm. I crouched down and kissed the top of Aidan's head.

The breeder handed us a certificate authenticating the fact that he was purebred and told us that he also came with a health guarantee. 'If there are any medical conditions within the next fourteen days, you can bring him back and I will give you a full refund,' she said.

Back in the van, I turned a movie on for the kids. Buster sat in a small box with a blanket on the floor of the backseat. 'How much did he cost?' I asked Jason, furious.

'Doesn't matter. I used my tips from the bar to pay for him.'

'Actually, it does matter. How much?'

'Twelve hundred.' He looked over at me.

'Are you fucking kidding me? You give me shit if I buy a $20 top and you go and spend $1200 on a dog? A dog that I didn't agree to?' I whispered.

'It's not the same. You spend too much, and that's why I give you shit. You have enough clothes; you don't need more.'

In the backseat, both kids were sleeping and the puppy was curled into a ball. 'That's bullshit,' I hissed. He ignored me. 'Fuck it. I'm not taking care of the dog. He's your responsibility. And you know what, you can use your tips to pay for all his expenses, too.' I turned the radio up and stared straight ahead.

This was one of the major conflicts in our marriage—finances. Jason wanted to pay our mortgage down as quickly as possible so we could have more financial freedom later in life. While I agreed that being mortgage-free would take pressure off us, I also wanted to enjoy our lives—to be able to go on vacation, eat out and splurge once in a while. Whenever I spent money without telling him, we would end up having screaming matches. Now that

I wasn't as vigilant about keeping the peace at home, our financial arguments became more frequent. It seemed the more I asserted my independence and didn't ask his permission before buying things, the more he tried to control our finances. This unilateral decision to spend such an exorbitant amount on a purebred dog made me feel like an afterthought in our marriage, as if what I wanted or didn't want were not important. He always expected I would just go along with his decisions in the end and not put up a fuss.

The puppy excitement was short-lived. After a week, one of Buster's eyes was red and bulging, swollen almost to the point of being shut. I called the vet and asked if they could check him, knowing we only had another week on the health guarantee from the breeder. I packed the kids and the puppy into the minivan, and off we went. The vet informed us that Buster had 'red-eye,' a condition common to his breed. He would need surgery, and 'typically, when it appears in one eye, it will spread to the other one.'

'How much is the surgery?' I asked.

'You're looking at about $2000 per eye. And there's no guarantee that it won't come back.'

I asked the vet to provide me with a document attesting to the fact that Buster had this medical condition. I then drove straight back to the breeder's place with the kids and the dog in the van. I pulled into the secluded driveway, pleased that I had been able to remember how to get there. I told the kids not to move and took the dog with me. I rang the doorbell, and when she answered I handed her the dog, along with the veterinarian's letter. The kids cried the whole way home. I turned the volume of the radio up to drown them out, and they eventually both fell asleep.

I never intended to upset them by taking the puppy back. But I felt as if I had been ambushed into getting a dog in the first place. While they enjoyed playing with Buster, at such a young age, I couldn't leave them alone for a minute with the dog without worrying that one of them might get hurt. They didn't understand that you can't just drop the puppy to the ground from waist level or push him off the sofa when you no longer want to play with him. I kept reminding them that if you try to take his toys away, he might bite you. Buster was an added stress to my already hectic life. I didn't want or need the added pressure of housebreaking a dog while potty-training my toddler. And so, I made a unilateral decision that was best for me.

When he got home from work that night, Jason woke me up.

'Where's the dog? He's not in his crate.'

'I took him back to the breeder.'

'What do you mean?'

'I mean, I took him to the vet to have his weird eye thing checked and he told me that the surgery would be around $2000. And that it would probably spread to the other eye.'

'Why didn't you call me?'

'Call you for what? Your phone is always turned off. The breeder said that he came with a health guarantee, so I took him back. I never agreed to a dog to begin with.'

'And what? I don't get a say in this?'

'No, you don't. You're never home anyway. I'm the one left dealing with the shit and piss everywhere.'

I took out the $1200 from my night table and handed it to him. 'Here. Your tips.'

I turned the lamp off and pulled the blankets up.

But that was not the end of Buster. Far from it.

For years, whenever we'd see a dog of the same breed, Jason would reminisce about our short time with the puppy, wishing we could have kept him. Jason never missed an opportunity to make sure the kids knew Mommy was the one who had taken the puppy away from them. I was forever the bad guy, the cruel mother who couldn't find it in her heart to let them keep their precious puppy.

Right here is where the narrative of a selfish, uncaring mother took root in my children's psyches.

It was easy then, in the years following my divorce from Jason, to turn me into the villain who broke the family.

It's the narrative I continue to fight against to this day.

Unfaithful

'I don't recognize you anymore. You used to be so beautiful and innocent,' Jason would often say. 'What happened to you?'

'Depression happened to me,' I'd snap back. In this back and forth of him wanting the 'old Sonia,' the submissive, soft-spoken wife, I found myself bubbling up like a volcano any time he was near me. My defenses were always raised, and I became like a scorpion waiting to attack.

Aside from these bursts of rage, the truth is, I had become numb to the world and the people around me. In this emotional state, I lost my moral compass. I found it difficult to feel and care about the impact of my words and actions. I was devastatingly lonely in my marriage, and without recognizing it, I found myself seeking validation from other men.

When I returned to work, I had a new boss who was young, handsome, funny and smart. John and I hit it off immediately. We had a similar sarcastic sense of humor, and we soon became close friends. Over lunch one day,

I opened up to him about my marital woes. He suggested I look outside of my marriage for the intimacy that was missing.

'It's just sex. It doesn't have to mean anything. Orgasms are good for you,' he'd said, laughing. This conversation lingered in my mind for a while, and the more I thought about it, the more I could justify it. I was craving intimacy and reckoned if I could get it elsewhere, maybe I could stay with Jason until the kids were older and I was more financially stable. That way, when I did leave, they might understand better and I wouldn't have to worry so much about being able to support them on my own.

That casual affair was good for me—it made me feel alive in ways I had forgotten. But it ended after a few months, preparing me for something much more wonderful to happen. Dustin came into my life six months after I returned to work. I was part of a small group planning a nationwide conference for tax practitioners. Each member was assigned specific keynote speakers from private sectors, and Dustin was mine. We started communicating over email and regular phone calls. He was polite, charming and funny. I still hadn't met him in person, but I had a feeling we would get on.

A month before the conference, Dustin was in Ottawa on a business trip and I'd organized a lunch meeting to go over the details of the conference. My boss had suggested I attend the lunch to answer any administrative questions. I saw Dustin sitting at a table in the dimly lit pub, wearing black jeans, a crisp white shirt and a sport jacket. I knew it was him because I'd asked him by text what he was wearing so I wouldn't embarrass myself by going up to the wrong person. He was a bit taller than me when he stood up to shake my hand. His light brown hair was parted to the side and his skin looked smooth and soft. His striking green eyes crinkled slightly when he smiled and tiny flecks of gold reflected from the candlelight on the table. John arrived and apologized for being late. We ordered our drinks and food and started discussing the logistics of the conference. I could feel Dustin's eyes on me and I delighted in it. When lunch ended, I gave him my personal cellphone number in case he needed to reach me during off-hours.

The next morning, he called to ask if I had time for a coffee. He was sitting at a small table in the hotel café with two mugs. He stood as soon as he saw me and pulled out the chair. We hugged briefly and I sat. He looked relaxed in his faded jeans and untucked blue button-down shirt. His eyes had more of a blue tint to them, I noticed, and the gold flecks were brighter. His shirt-sleeves were rolled up and his forearms looked strong. He slid the mug over, and when I reached out our hands touched. Electricity ran through my body.

We talked about our families, our home lives, growing up, and work. He told me that while he'd been born in Ottawa, his father had been in the military and that they had moved around a lot. They'd lived in Germany for five years before being posted in Saskatchewan. He had chosen to remain there when his parents returned to Ottawa. When his father suddenly passed away from a heart attack at forty-five, an eighteen-year-old Dustin decided to move back in with his mom. Sharing our histories was natural and easy. I told him how I'd grown up in a small town and had desperately wanted to escape it. I talked about my parents, the daycare and how I'd been around kids my whole life. I opened up to him about my postpartum depression and how much I struggled to feel a connection with my baby girl.

'What's that like?' he asked. 'My wife didn't have that with our kids.'

'It's hard to explain. It's like being lost in a thick fog. Your mind plays tricks on you. In the worst of it, I had some scary, fucked-up thoughts. I was in a really dark place.'

'Do you still feel like that?'

'No, not with the antidepressants. I just feel numb. Not happy, but not sad.'

I told him about Brooke Shields' book. 'If you're curious to know what postpartum depression feels like, you should read that book.'

I looked at my watch and saw that over two hours had passed. We stood and hugged, this time holding on a little bit longer. His body was strong, pressed up against mine. I felt warm all over. Pulling away, our faces close, I wanted him to lean in for a kiss. He didn't.

The next time we spoke he told me that he had gone to the bookstore across the street after our coffee date and bought Brooke Shields's *Down Came the Rain*. 'I read it on the plane on the way back to Calgary.'

'So, what did you think?'

'Well, I'm sorry that you're going through that. And I think that your husband is a damn fool for not reading it.'

After hanging up, I sat and wondered why he had read the book. I found it odd, yet charming, that someone I had just met would be interested in better understanding what I was going through. I couldn't grasp how a man who had no real investment in me or my life would want to know more about my mental well-being than my own husband did. I felt seen and validated, worthy of attention for the first time in a long time. And I was quickly captivated by that feeling.

Dustin started calling me on his way to work every morning. There was a two-hour time difference, so I would be at my desk when he was driving. I started looking forward to these daily calls and told him as much. He admitted that he really enjoyed them, too. Our communications started spilling into the evenings, after I'd put the kids to bed. We never seemed to run out of things to talk about. The more I opened up to Dustin, the more I withdrew from Jason.

Dustin and I got into the habit of chatting most weeknights once the kids were asleep. I knew what I was doing was wrong, but it felt good to be seen, heard and admired. I was less tense and more playful, which made me a better, more relaxed mother to my kids. In this state, I didn't feel as if I was taking any aspects of myself away from Aidan and Cassie. I wondered what might happen if Jason found out that I was forming a relationship with another man, but even that wasn't enough to deter me from feeling happiness, connection and a sense of freedom outside my marriage. I was of two minds, and I could separate Sonia the mother from Sonia the woman.

A month later, standing at the front of the Conference Hall in Victoria with the other organizers, I watched as Dustin got out of the cab, smiled and waved. My body lit up with tingles of excitement. I showed him to his hotel room and handed him the keys and a conference binder.

'I will be in that meeting room if you need anything else,' I said, pointing down the hallway. 'Dinner is at 7:30 p.m., but cocktails start at 6:30 if you're interested.'

'Are you going to the cocktail hour?' he asked.

I smiled. 'As one of the organizers, my attendance is expected at every event for the next three days. Someone has to entertain all of you tax geeks,' I continued. He burst out laughing and I took a small bow and headed to my meeting room. I still had a few tasks to finish up before getting ready for the cocktail hour. I was cleaning up a couple of hours later when I heard a knock at the door. Dustin asked if I could scan and email a document to him. Standing at the printer, I could feel his eyes on me. I took my time leaning over my computer at the table, reveling in how it felt to be desired.

We glanced at each other from across the room during cocktail hour. I had arranged the seating for the dinner and had placed him next to me at our table. Every time his hand or leg would touch mine, my entire body lit up. When the evening ended, Dustin followed me to my room. I woke the next morning with his arms wrapped around me. I hadn't expected him to spend the night. He looked peaceful in the sunlight, and my heart skipped a beat.

I knew he was married. And I was cheating on my husband.

Yet when we were together, I came alive in ways I needed for my psychic survival. I grappled with my guilt. But my own needs for love and happiness won.

We continued to speak several times daily and found ways to be together every time he was in town. Because the Federal Tax Authority was in Ottawa, he often had to travel for meetings and we would plan to see each other during the day. While our relationship was physical every chance we got, it was the emotional side of it that kept us longing for one another. As months went by, my feelings for him deepened. We would lie in our post-sex bliss, limbs intertwined, my head resting on his chest as I listened to his heart beat, and dream of a life when these moments wouldn't be stolen, but rather our reality.

I began to glimpse happiness. And I didn't need any pills to feel it. I knew what we were doing was wrong, and I felt immense guilt over how this would impact our loved ones. I tried hard to separate the 'us' when we were together from the individuals we were with our families. We both had entire lives outside of the bubble we created when we were together, and in these fleeting moments, all we focused on was how incredible it felt to be seen for who we truly were without pretense, obligation or fear of being rejected. And even though the remorse would inevitably creep in when we went our separate ways, we were hooked on each other and couldn't stay apart for very long. As much pain as I knew our growing relationship might eventually cause, I didn't want to put a stop to it.

I had found true love.

We both had.

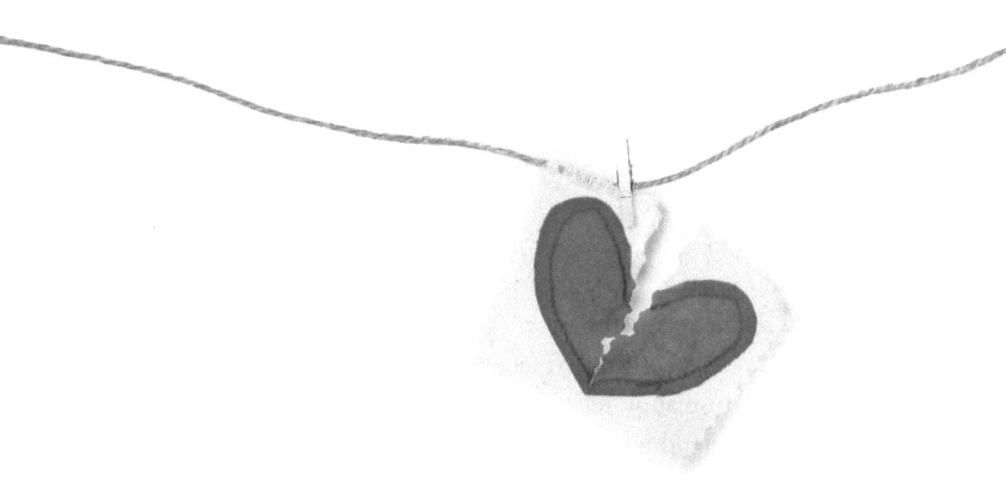

An End and a Beginning

Almost a year after the conference, I travelled to Vancouver for another week-long work trip. I hated leaving the kids, but I was looking forward to some alone-time. A few days into the trip I decided that, once I got home, I was going to tell Jason I wanted a divorce. I couldn't keep waiting for the right time. There is, it seems, no 'right time' to end your marriage.

The flight back to Ottawa felt never-ending. I sat looking out of the window, listening to my music, wondering if I was about to make the biggest mistake or best decision of my life. I wondered how the kids would adjust to having divorced parents. I worried they would get stuck in the middle, feeling forced to choose one parent over the other. I didn't know how Jason would react when I told him. I hoped that once he had time to take in my decision, we'd find a way to move forward that would minimize the impact on Aidan and Cassie, and to co-parent in a respectful manner. I wanted us to both put the kids first.

I wiped away my tears as the plane landed. I wasn't happy in my marriage; I hadn't been for years. Jason and I were completely disconnected. We had become two strangers barely coexisting. We argued often and loudly, and I worried about the kids hearing us. I dreaded weekends when we would all be together. I knew that it wasn't enough for me to 'stay for the kids.' I was concerned that having them grow up in a tense household with a deeply unhappy mother would be more detrimental in the long term. I simply could not keep pretending for the sake of giving them two parents under one roof. I needed more. I wanted to live a life of love and passion, not resentment and pretense.

I saw them as I came down the escalator. Cassie looked so small, holding Jason's hand. Aidan had a big grin, flowers cradled in his arms, and my heart sank. The kids ran to me, and I knelt and hugged them tightly, breathing them in. Jason took a step forward to kiss me. I put my hand on his chest and turned my cheek to him. I didn't want him showing me affection when there was no tenderness left between us. I saw no need to pretend. As we walked out of the arrivals terminal, the winter air on my face matched the chill in my heart. Right then, I knew I was making the right decision.

The kids asked a million questions on the way home. *How was Vancouver? Was it cold? Is there snow? What's an airplane like? Were you scared it might crash? Is there food on a plane? How do they cook the food on the plane?*

Their questions were a perfect distraction. As long as they kept coming I didn't have to talk to Jason. Once home, we ordered pizza and watched a movie. Cassie sat in my lap and Aidan leaned hard against me, his hand in mine. Every now and then, he'd squeeze it three times. *I. Love. You.* I'd squeeze back four and he'd smile, trying to inch closer. When the movie ended, I put the kids to bed.

'Don't leave us anymore, Mommy, okay?' Aidan asked, his big blue eyes looking deeply into mine.

'Okay,' I said, kissing his forehead. 'I won't.'

He smiled and my chest tightened. Because I felt as if I was lying to him.

As parents, we all lie to our children at one point or another. We make up stories about Santa Claus, the Tooth Fairy and the Easter Bunny. We tell ourselves that all we are doing is safeguarding their innocence as long as we can. We want them to believe that the world is full of magic and assume they're too young to understand the truth. We even debate the age at which we should come clean about all these small lies. I must have expected that this 'lie,' just like the one about Santa Claus, would be forgiven. I believed my kids would eventually understand that, in order for me to maintain my sanity, I had to end my marriage.

And I knew this would completely change my children's worlds. The only life they knew would be pulled apart. I didn't know how long it would take for us to find a new normal. But I could no longer continue to live in the house that held so much darkness for me and in which I had suffered silently for years. Would my initiating this new era be seen as me 'leaving'? Surely other women had left their unhappy marriages without losing their children's trust? As I blew Aidan a kiss and closed his door halfway, I vowed I would find a way to make sure my children knew I was not abandoning them.

I leaned on the wall and took a deep breath. The TV was loud in the living room. I bit the inside of my cheek.

Now.

Do it now.

I sat on the sofa facing Jason. He glanced at me and returned his attention to the show he was watching.

I cleared my throat. 'Jason, I need to talk to you.'

He sat with his knees tucked underneath him. He turned the volume down, placed the remote control on his lap and crossed his arms over his chest. He turned to face me. His eyes were cold. *Ah, there you are.* Now I recognized him.

'Okay. Talk.'

I swallowed hard. 'I don't want to be married anymore. I want a divorce.' I heard the words come out of my mouth but couldn't be sure that I had said them out loud. I blinked a few times, and his face came into focus. He looked deflated, like I'd punched him in the gut. He clenched his jaw, returning his gaze to the TV screen, blinking rapidly.

I continued. 'I'm not happy. We're not happy. We haven't been happy for a long time now.'

'I knew this was coming. I could tell. I knew it right away when I saw you at the airport.'

'Jason, I just, I can't ke—'

'Why? Why do you say that I'm not happy? I am happy, Sonia.' He untucked his legs and shifted in his seat. 'Sure, things aren't perfect right now, but we can work through it,' he insisted.

I shook my head. 'No, we can't. We can't work through it.' I rubbed my forehead and looked down at the floor.

'Why? Tell me why.' His eyes were burning my skin. 'What about the kids? Do you have any idea how much of an impact this will have on them?'

He took off his glasses and wiped his eyes. 'Jesus, Sonia. Why are you doing this? How can I change your mind? Tell me what to do and I'll do it. I'll do whatever you want …'

I couldn't bring myself to look at him—pleading, wanting to make me happy, willing to do whatever it took. I had not seen this side of him in years. Why couldn't he have been more like this when I was in my darkest moments? Why couldn't he have shown his vulnerability then?

'Mommy?' I heard Aidan coming down the hallway. I hurried off the sofa, grabbed his hand and turned him around. Too late; he'd seen his father crying. God knows how much he'd heard.

'Aidan, honey, it's bedtime, come on.' I pulled him by the hand back to his room. 'Mommy and Daddy are having a grown-up talk.'

His eyes searched mine. 'Why is Daddy crying? Did you make him sad?' I picked him up and sat him on his bed, kneeling in front of him.

I stroked his chubby cheek gently. 'Daddy is a little bit sad right now, but he'll be okay. I promise. Everything'll be okay. Time for bed.' I kissed him hard as tears pooled in the corners of my eyes. I walked away before they could fall.

When I returned to the sofa, Jason asked, 'Do you still love me?'

I hesitated. I knew I was hurting him, but I didn't want to lie. I was exhausted from all the years of not telling the truth—to him and to myself. 'No. I don't. I haven't loved you for a long time.' I paused. 'I'm not entirely sure I ever really did.' My words felt sharp, like glass shards in my mouth.

He stood quickly, shaken. 'I need some air.' He grabbed his cigarettes and his jacket and stepped outside.

I watched him pace up and down the driveway. He leaned back on the car and exhaled, thick smoke surrounding him. I heard my phone ping and walked down the stairs.

1 new message from DB: *Hope you're doing ok.*

I put the phone in my purse and returned to the sofa. Jason came back inside and stood next to me. I looked up hesitantly.

'Okay,' he said, resigned. 'If this is what you want. But I want you to know that this is not what I want. I want us to work this out. For the kids' sakes. For our family.'

I stood to face him. 'I'm so sorry,' I said, reaching out to touch his arm. He pulled away and walked to the kitchen. I watched him take out a notebook from the drawer.

'Let's figure out who gets what,' he said, pushing past me.

'Seriously?' I shook my head. 'This is what you want to do right now? Divide the assets?' I don't know why I was surprised; with Jason, everything had always about the bottom line. We spent the next hour going through who would get what, right down to the silverware and tea towels. I wanted to sell the house. He insisted that one of us should keep it. 'Continuity for the kids,' he said. 'I'll buy you out. They'll need some stability if we want them to get through this. You have no idea how hard this will be for them.'

'I think if we explain it to them together, they will understand. A lot of their friends at school and daycare have parents who are separated.'

We agreed to shared custody. We both signed the sheet of paper. 'I think this is what's best. For all of us,' I said.

He clenched his jaw. 'I don't. I think that the kids having two parents under one roof is what's best for all of us. I'm going to sleep on the sofa tonight.' He turned the TV back on and returned his focus to the screen.

That was it. Like ripping off a Band-Aid. I had said the words, and there they sat, a gaping wound exposed. I don't know what I expected him to say or how I wanted him to react. We felt so far apart that I had assumed he would agree we weren't happy and that it would be best to go our separate ways. I was unprepared for his denial and for his willingness to live such a desperate existence in a marriage that surely was not fulfilling him. If I was so unhappy, how could he be happy? Wasn't part of a marriage's contract for both parties to be invested in each other's joys, and to try to understand and support them through their sorrows? Why would he want to go on living the way we were? Why would he expect that I would continue to suffer only to give the kids two parents under one roof? What message would we be passing on to our children if they grew up with parents who resented each other? Why did he seem so insistent that my unhappiness was less important than keeping the family together? He still refused to discuss my depression and the impact it was having on all of us, and I could no longer ignore how deserted I felt in our union. I didn't have it in me to continue merely existing; I wanted to live a life filled with joy, laughter and kindness. I was worn out from all the strain and hostility that plagued our moments together as a family.

And still, I understood where Jason was coming from. We were both raised by parents who believed that marriage is for life. You pick a person, build a family and home with them, and you endure all of the storms. Together. Even when there is no love left. I guess you hold on, hoping the love might find its way back. My parents' generation and the ones before that chose to love in a straight line. They took the 'forever' part to heart. You stay for the children, to give them a true sense of family. But I could not do that. I did not want my children to grow up with parents who didn't love each other. Maybe, in his own way, Jason did love me. But not in the way that I needed him to, not in the way I wanted to be loved. Now, my kids were about to be stuck in a love triangle. Getting pulled from all sides, never really knowing where they belonged. It was a sickening choice.

I turned back to Jason before going into the bedroom. 'We should probably tell them sooner rather than later. Aidan already knows that something is up. He saw you crying earlier.'

'No. We don't tell them anything until we have a plan. This will be hard enough. I don't want to add any confusion,' he answered without looking at me. He turned the volume up and I closed the bedroom door.

Staring at the ceiling, I cried, for me and for Jason; for the pain my decision would bring upon Aidan and Cassie; for tearing apart the only world they had ever known. I cried, knowing that their lives would be forever changed. I also cried tears of relief for finding the courage to do what I knew in my heart was the right thing.

And although our lives would look very different moving forward, I really did believe that it would eventually be better for all of us.

I couldn't have been more mistaken.

The People We Lean On

I woke the next morning tired and jet-lagged. Jason was already up, feeding the kids. His eyes were puffy and red. We tiptoed around each other, barely uttering a word. After breakfast, he announced that he was going to visit his parents.

'Me too, Daddy, I wanna go see Granny,' Aidan piped up.

He knelt down beside him. 'Not today, buddy. Daddy has to talk to Granny and Grandad. Grown-up talk.'

Aidan looked to me and I forced a smile. 'Come on, why don't we go to the park.'

A few hours later, Jason returned, slamming the front door behind him. I heard his footsteps stomping down to the basement. I turned up the cartoons we were watching and followed him down.

'Jason, what's wrong? What's happened?'

'What do you care?' he shouted.

'Keep your voice down,' I said, pointing up the stairs.

'We need to separate our bank accounts. I'm going to need to be careful with my expenses if I keep the house,' he continued, talking more to himself than to me.

'You don't have to keep the house. We can sell it.'

He shook his head. 'No. The kids need this house. It's their home.'

I sighed and turned to leave. He grabbed my arm. 'Why are you doing this? The truth this time.'

I pulled away, confused. 'What do you mean? I told you last night. I don't love you anymore.'

'I don't believe you. You don't stop loving someone overnight. There's something you're not telling me.'

I felt a rush of heat to my cheeks and stormed up the stairs before he could notice. The close bond that Dustin and I had been building for the last year had helped me realize how unfulfilling my marriage was. And the passion we shared whenever we were together further emphasized what I'd known for a long time: I did not love Jason. My love for him hadn't disappeared overnight. It had been bleeding out for years. I couldn't continue putting on the false front of the happy family we pretended to be. I wanted more for myself, for my kids and for him. I wanted a love rooted in mutual kindness, respect and compassion. These were qualities our marriage never truly had. And I hoped that with time, he would come to realize this as well.

•••

The next day, I drove to my parents' house. I wanted to be the one to tell them, and I didn't trust him not to speak to them before I had the chance to.

'Why would you do that?' my dad asked, not waiting for an answer. 'You both have good jobs, a nice new house, happy, healthy kids. Why throw it all away?'

I felt like I was being scolded. I looked to my mom for support. She shook her head with disappointment, and once again I felt like a child misbehaving. Here I was, their perfect daughter, letting them down once more, the way I had when I'd snuck out of our house to go to the bar with my friends and got caught. Or the time I got drunk on peach schnapps, underage, and threw up in the ditch by the driveway. I felt the same shame boiling up in me as I had the day I told them I was quitting university. And now, here I was, adding yet another stain to our family tapestry.

'I'm not happy. I haven't been happy in a long time.' I looked at them pleadingly. 'Please, please try to understand. You've seen it yourself. We don't agree on spending, or how to parent the kids.' My mom looked at the floor. I continued, 'We barely talk to each other. He's always working nights. He's never home, and I've pretty much been raising the kids on my own.'

My dad huffed, stood up and left the room. This conversation was over. I looked at my mom. She stepped forward and pulled me in for a hug. 'You're making a mistake,' she whispered in my ear before kissing my cheek and going after my dad. I grabbed my car keys and left, admonished for choosing my own happiness. I drove away more dejected than I had ever been.

'Your parents think you're making a mistake.' I felt a shiver run up my spine hearing Jason's voice behind me. I was standing in the kitchen looking out into the backyard, replaying my earlier conversation with them.

'What did you just say?' I asked, glancing over my shoulder. I turned, glaring at him. 'You called my parents?'

'No, I texted your mom and then she called me. They wanted to hear my side of it.'

'Why? Why would you possibly think that they would want your side of it? You're not their blood.' I felt betrayed as he slowly strode toward me.

'I've always gotten along well with your parents, Sonia. I wanted them to know that I don't agree with this decision. I told them that I want us to work it out. And guess what? They agree with me.'

I was speechless.

The walls felt like they were closing in. I couldn't believe my parents had spoken to him behind my back and were choosing to side with him. I wanted to scream. The fire in my belly was too much to keep in.

'Yeah, well, they don't get a vote in this,' I shouted, slamming my hand down on the kitchen counter.

Monday morning couldn't come fast enough. I drove the kids to school and daycare, grateful that the weekend was finally over. I assumed that Jason was working his usual evening shift. I could not wait to get out of the house and away from him.

I sat at my desk and John came out to greet me with a goofy grin on his face. 'Hey! How was Vancouver? You still married?' He chuckled. This was an ongoing joke with him since I'd told him that things weren't going well at home. I leaned back in my chair and looked up at him.

'Actually, no.'

He laughed, thinking I was joking. My eyes welled up with tears and he waved me into his office, closing the door. 'Tell me what happened. The short version.'

I gave him the abbreviated story. His only advice was, 'Get yourself a lawyer. Now.'

I went back to my desk and saw an email from Dustin. He'd reached out to a friend at a law firm and explained my situation, saying that I would need legal advice quickly. His friend made some calls and arranged for me to meet with a lawyer that same afternoon.

Sitting across from the lawyer, I handed over the sheet Jason and I had drawn up and signed on the weekend. 'This is how we would like to divide the assets.'

'This is a good start, but you can't physically move out until you have a signed separation agreement. If you do, the Court will consider that you have given up your rights to the property, assets and custody of the children.'

'How long will that take?' I asked. He shrugged his shoulders, handing me back the piece of paper. 'Depends on how long he wants to drag his feet.'

I left the lawyer's office feeling deflated.

•••

When I arrived at Aidan's school for pick-up, I was informed that his dad had already collected him. I called Cassie's daycare, and he had also picked her up. I rushed to the house, a feeling of dread spreading through my body. I could hear muffled sounds coming from the playroom in the basement. I hurried down the stairs, around the corner, and saw Cassie playing with her toys on the floor. Aidan and Jason were on the daybed. Jason was lying down, his head on a pillow, crying. Aidan was gently stroking his hair, trying to soothe him.

I struggled to register what I was seeing. This couldn't be real. I picked Cassie up briskly. I looked at Jason and barked, 'Get up. Now.' He sat up slowly, and I grabbed Aidan by the hand. I took both kids up the stairs and turned on a cartoon with the volume louder than I normally would allow.

Aidan looked up at me. 'Daddy's sad.'

I stroked his cheek. 'I know, baby. I know.' I kissed the top of his head and he turned his gaze to the TV screen.

In the basement, I closed the playroom door. Jason was sitting up, wiping his tears. He put his glasses on and looked at me. I felt like I was going to explode.

'What the hell are you doing? Why aren't you at work?' I asked, livid.

He looked at me coldly. 'I called my boss and told him what happened. He told me to take a sick day.'

'Jason. Do you have any idea how messed up this is? Aidan is already such a worrier. I can't believe you would you cry in front of him. Let alone have him console you!' I said crossly. I stood in front of him with my hands on my hips. 'We haven't even told them what is going on. Do you know how confus—'

'I told them,' he said, his tone flat. 'I told them that you're leaving us. That you don't want to be part of our family anymore.'

My body started shaking. 'What. The. Fuck?' No, this wasn't happening. I paced around the small room. 'Why would you talk to them without me?' The heat was rising in my body. 'I am NOT leaving them, Jason,' I shouted. 'I'm leaving YOU. Not the kids. How could you do this?'

'How could *I* do this?' he said, standing up. He pointed to me. '*You're* doing this. Not me. *You're* the one leaving, taking away the only family they've ever known. All I did was tell them the truth.'

'That is not the truth. For fuck sakes, Jason. I can't believe this.' I leaned on the wall and put my face in my hands. I was so furious that I couldn't breathe. 'You can't do this,' I said, shaking my head. 'You can't lean on him like that. He's a child. A four-year-old child. I won't let you do this to him.'

I crouched down, feeling unsteady. I was trying to keep myself from hitting him. I shook my head, fisting my hands and clenching my jaw. I looked up and glared at him.

He sat on the floor across from me and hugged his knees into his chest. 'I didn't mean to cry in front of them, Sonia. I can't help it. I'm heartbroken over this.' He paused and wiped his nose on his sleeve. 'I'm sorry that I can't keep it together like you. I didn't ask for this. You spring this on me and expect that I'll be okay with it. I'm not. I am broken. Can't you see that?'

He was disheveled, unshaven, and looked like he hadn't showered in days. His eyes were puffy and red, with circles underneath that were dark and deep. I stood and shook my head in disgust. Leaving the playroom, I turned back to him and said, 'I met with a lawyer today. I gave him a copy of the list we made on Friday night. He's starting the paperwork. Let's just get this over with.'

I don't think that I will ever be able to properly articulate the avalanche of feelings that overcame me as I walked into that playroom. To see our kids, so little, being forced to carry the burden of their father's sadness enraged me. I knew that we could not continue to live under one roof without severely damaging our children. I started to see the heaviness of Jason's pain spilling into Aidan's eyes. Almost like he felt a responsibility to make his father happy and whole again.

Mommy broke Daddy's heart. Mommy broke the family. Mommy left us. Mommy abandoned us. These words, like a nursery rhyme, were repeated over and over again to my children. In that one move, I was ambushed. Perhaps it was Jason's way of retaliating because he claimed he didn't see the breakdown of our marriage coming. And that is exactly why I couldn't stay—he was unwilling or unable to see or support me in the ways I needed. This was his way of punishing me for asserting my right to be happy. This was his way of controlling the narrative. He would forever be the victim, and I, the enemy.

Now, I look back at that moment and wonder if I should have fought back. Maybe I should have tried to explain my truth to the kids, tell them my side of the story. But they were so young, so innocent, victims of circumstances, without a voice. I didn't want to add to their already heavy burden.

So, I stayed silent, as I had learned to do before when I had been ambushed by someone I trusted. I thought it would make matters worse if I tried to explain grown-up feelings to small children.

In doing this, I made it easy for them to decide who the villain was.

Downsizing

I liked the place right away. It was a second-level apartment in a triplex. The front steps were concrete and wide; the space itself was bright and clean. It had a little balcony in the back, big enough to put a grill and maybe a small table with a couple of chairs. It overlooked a shared yard, which backed onto a biking trail and a little creek. The yard wasn't fenced, and I wondered if Cassie might venture off and fall into the water. She had a natural curiosity and fearlessness that made me uneasy. The word 'no' meant nothing to her; if she wanted to do something, she would.

The floor plan was similar to the marital home I was soon to vacate. Up the stairs to the main door. Living room, dining room and kitchen to the right. Master, bathroom and kids' bedrooms to the left. Their respective rooms were even on the same sides. One was painted blue, the other pink. The couple moving out had a son and daughter. I took the application and the landlord's business card and told him I'd be in touch soon.

Even though we didn't have a signed separation agreement yet, I had decided to start looking for a place to live. I couldn't handle being under the same roof with Jason much longer. He had taken to writing me letters because he claimed it was easier for him to express himself this way. We rarely spoke, and when we did, it inevitably turned into screaming and insult-hurling matches. The letters were all the same: he didn't believe that I didn't love him. He wanted to know why I was doing this. He wanted to know how he could change my mind.

I would become exasperated, not wanting to rehash the same topics over and over again. He would accuse me of not allowing him to feel his pain. I would blame him for dragging his feet. He wanted us to try again. I wanted out now. Push and pull, like being swept away at sea, slowly drowning.

•••

I sat at the dining room table and filled out the application form. I wasn't sure what banking information to use, as all our finances were still joint. I made a mental note to open a new account the next day. I didn't know what date to put as 'move-in.' I felt stuck. Like I was in quicksand. I didn't want to stay, but I didn't know how to leave. I settled on April 1st. Maybe if I had a move-out date, Jason would accept that I was serious and sign the papers.

'Thanks for picking these up,' I said, handing the landlord the application and deposit of two months' rent.

I leaned in the doorway, hugging myself. The air was crisp, and I could see my breath. I looked at my watch. Almost 9 p.m. Jason would be back soon from his darts league. Probably best to go to bed before he got home. I locked the front door and turned the porch light on. Walking into the bedroom, I saw his car headlights flooding the driveway. *Please, dear God, let it be a peaceful night.* These words became I prayer I repeated every night as I went to bed.

But there were no more peaceful nights to come. Only more letters, more tears and small children crawling into my bed. I knew that as long as we shared a house, there would be no peace.

What I didn't know then is that, no matter our living arrangements, there would never be peace again.

Those were dark days, and I am grateful to be past them. With the grace of hindsight, I have been able to look back on those letters Jason wrote me. I recently sat outside with my coffee mug in the early morning light and re-read them. Time changes perspective. Back then, I was blind to his pain. Of course, I didn't want to acknowledge it. I was carrying my own burdens of guilt and sadness. To move forward, I had to continue to see him as the person who failed to support me when I was at my lowest. I didn't want to see how my decision had impacted him. I wanted to carve him out of my life completely. I expected he would move on with his because I was moving on with mine. Perhaps I didn't give him the time he needed to process the grief of losing his wife.

Many years later, I read those letters more kindly, allowing his feelings to wash over me, as if they were my own. I was brought back into the push and pull of his anger and sadness, the back and forth of his emotions. If only I had been more compassionate. Maybe then we might have been able to create a better co-parenting relationship. Maybe our kids wouldn't have been caught in the crossfire. Maybe my son would not have shut me out of his life.

But there are some things we can never know. When we are living through dark times, we can't foresee the impact our decisions, words or behaviors will have on others. In the middle of the storm, all we can do is protect ourselves and do whatever is necessary to survive. Once the tempest has passed, we might get the chance to ask for forgiveness for the wrongs we have done and hope that someday it will be granted.

But even then, there are no guarantees it will be.

Get Out

'What are you doing with my wallet?' I cried.

I'd walked into the kitchen to find Jason had pulled all the cards from my wallet and was searching the compartments.

I ripped it out of his hands, picking my cards, cash, coins and scraps of paper up from the countertop.

'What's this?' he asked, holding up a scrap of paper. He opened it up and read the words scribbled in red ink, *You look beautiful today.*

I felt my cheeks burning as I recognized the note that Dustin had slipped me during a meeting at one point. I'd forgotten I had tucked it into my wallet over a year ago.

'It's just a note that someone gave me at the office.'

'Who? Who gave you this?' he said, throwing it at me. I picked it up and put it in my pocket.

'I don't have to answer that question. You have no right to go through my wallet. Or my purse. Or my phone. We are not together anymore.'

I was furious that he continued to invade my privacy and refused to respect my boundaries. But I was guilt-ridden, knowing I was keeping my affair with Dustin a secret from him. I desperately wanted my separation from Jason to be kept apart from my relationship with Dustin. I knew that Jason wasn't accepting my explanations for wanting a divorce, and I didn't want to give him something outside of our broken marriage on which to lay the blame. Had there been no Dustin, our marriage would still have ended.

I had already explained to the kids what was going to happen. Mommy would move into a new house and Daddy would keep the one we lived in now. I had printed a calendar and taped it to the refrigerator. Each night before bed, we would cross out the day that had just ended. When the days were all crossed out, Mommy would move out. This would be the beginning of living one week with Daddy and one week with Mommy. They seemed to understand how this would work. Many of the kids at school and daycare also had two homes. Aidan said that his friends liked having two of everything, especially video games and favorite toys. I made a mental note to not indulge in twos-of-everything.

After the wallet incident, I started to keep my purse and phone in the bedroom at night. But I would still sometimes wake up to find my phone locked out and my purse contents all over the floor. When I'd confront Jason, he'd deny responsibility or claim he had the right to know what his wife was up to. One Saturday afternoon, he walked in while I was on the phone with Dustin. I turned around and ended the call quickly.

'Who were you talking to?' he asked.

'None of your business,' I said, looking away. 'I thought you were spending the day at your parents' place?'

'Changed my mind. Besides, last I checked, this is my house too.'

I didn't want to fight with him. 'Whatever. The kids are having a nap. I'm going to have a shower.'

I locked the bathroom door and turned the shower on. I had just put the kids down and figured I could take my time. Jason could handle it if they woke up. I was rinsing the shampoo out of my hair when suddenly the shower door flew open.

'What is this?' Jason asked, holding my cellphone up.

I wiped my eyes, confused. How did he get in? I had locked the door. He was holding a small pin in his other hand. 'Did you pick the lock? Get out. Get out,' I yelled, trying to close the shower door.

He held it open with his elbow and turned the phone screen on. 'What the fuck is this?'

I looked at the screen. **1 new message from DB:** *I love you.*

I tried to cover up my naked body, filled with shame. He dropped the phone on the bathmat. 'I love you? I love you? How could you do this to me. To us,' he said, pointing to the kids' bedrooms. He stormed out, slamming the door behind him.

•••

I stood there, with the shower door wide open, water splashing onto the floor. I turned the faucet off and reached for a towel. My eyes welled with tears, which dropped to the floor. I caught a glimpse of myself in the mirror, and the haunted look in my eyes instantly took me back to one of the most painful moments in my life.

At seventeen, I had moved out of my parents' house and was volunteering as a camera-person with a television production crew covering sporting events. My roommate had helped me get the gig, and I loved it. One day, I was filming a baseball match from the opposing team dugout. Throughout the game, a cute guy in the stands seemed to be trying to get my attention. He'd leaned over and asked my name.

'If you can find me after the game, I'll tell you,' I flirted. We would be a while clearing all of our equipment and I fully expected he wouldn't hang around. More than an hour after the game had ended, as we were leaving, I saw him waiting by the stadium doors. He asked me out on a date that evening and I agreed, won over by his charm and persistence. We went out for pizza and agreed to meet up for coffee the next day. Although I hadn't been interested in meeting anyone new, he was so attentive and charismatic that he won me over in no time. Stephen quickly inserted himself into my life.

It didn't take long to realize that he was the jealous type. At first, I naively found it adorable that he didn't like it when other guys talked to me. He then started showing up unexpectedly when I was out with my friends. He always insisted on saying goodnight before I went to bed, 'So your voice is the last thing I hear before I fall asleep,' he'd say. I thought it was cute, but his behavior should have been a huge red flag. He had a temper and always had to have his arm around me when we were out in public. His overbearing behavior should have made me nervous. But I wanted so badly to be loved that I ignored my gut feeling that this relationship was moving too fast and in a treacherous direction.

Stephen and I had been dating for a few months when I decided that I was ready for him to meet my parents. We drove to their house on a Friday evening and decided to stay overnight to avoid the long drive back into town. I convinced my parents that I was mature enough to share the sofa-bed with him. After all, I was living on my own in the city.

And that is how it happened. My first sexual experience is one I will never forget, because I did not consent. My boyfriend held me down forcefully and took something of mine I didn't want to give. I said *no*. I said *stop*. I tried to push him off, but he was much stronger. I didn't scream for help; I didn't fight harder. I froze. I lay there, crying and staring at the dim green neon light of the clock on the oven, watching it change as the minutes went by. A steady stream of tears rolled out of my eyes until he was done. He got off me and I pulled my underwear and shorts back on. I rolled onto my side, paralyzed. I didn't leave the sofa-bed, I didn't run into the shower to erase what had been done to me. I simply turned around and closed my eyes. I told myself that it was my fault. I deserved it. It was the price I had to pay for insisting on sharing the sofa-bed with him. I obviously had been putting out the vibe that this is what I wanted. I had begged my parents to finally see me as an adult and let me sleep in the same room as my boyfriend. My brother had been allowed to share a bed with his girlfriend for years, and I wanted equal treatment.

The next morning, I got up early and had *that* shower. I scrubbed myself so hard with scalding water that I thought my skin would peel off. I still felt dirty. I took inventory of the bruises on my wrists and arms from where he'd pinned me down; the bruises in my inner thighs where he'd pried my legs open with his knee. As I looked at my reflection, I realized that none of this was my fault. He had *raped* me. The word made me feel sick to my stomach. But I didn't know what to do. I couldn't tell my parents; my father would have killed him with his bare hands.

After brunch with my family, we drove in silence and I recoiled as far as I could from his reach. When we got to my apartment, I mustered all the courage I had and said, 'It's over. This, this thing is done. If you try to come near me, I'll go to the police and press charges on you for raping me.'

He grabbed my arm when I reached for the car door. 'What the hell are you talking about? I didn't rape you. We had sex. And you enjoyed it.'

I pulled away, shaking, and stood outside the car. 'How can you possibly think that I enjoyed it? I told you to stop! I cried the whole time.'

'Bullshit, you're a fucking cock-tease. Just 'cause you regret letting me pop your cherry doesn't make me a rapist.'

Before slamming the car door, I said, 'I mean it, Stephen, if you even try to get near me I'm going to the police.'

He rolled down his window, threw an empty soda can at me and yelled, 'You were a lousy lay, you fucking bitch,' as he sped away. I stood in the driveway, staring at his taillights in the distance. I dropped to the ground, shaking and sobbing. I picked up the empty can and dropped it in the recycle bin beside the door.

My roommate, Marianne, took one look at me and knew something was wrong. I broke down and told her everything. She cried with me and insisted that I call the police. I said, 'No, I just want it to go away and pretend like it didn't happen.' I made her promise that we would never bring it up again.

A few days later, she came home late from work and looked at me differently. Stephen had been waiting outside her workplace and wanted to tell her what really happened. She told me that his version of events sounded more likely to be true. She seemed convinced that I had made up this rape story to get sympathy and attention. She asked why I didn't scream for help, why I lay next to him after he "raped" me. Why I didn't tell my parents the next morning? Why I had insisted that we never bring it up again?

Her line of questioning made me feel sick to my stomach. How could she take his word over mine? What kind of person did she think I was, to make up such a horrendous story? The way she looked at me confirmed what I'd have to do. It was becoming more and more clear that we weren't going able to continue sharing an apartment. I had trusted her with my pain, shared my most agonizing experience, allowed myself to be vulnerable, and she was now standing in front of me saying, *I don't believe you.*

...

I moved out a few weeks later. I couldn't stand to be around her, knowing she thought I'd made it all up. Her behavior taught me that when terrible things happen, I could not rely on people to believe me. She reinforced my feelings of isolation at one of the lowest points in my life. Someone I had trusted and confided in had dismissed my pain and sided with the person who had hurt me. I became one of those women we read about in the news—society rarely believes a rape victim, especially if the people involved in the nonconsensual sex are dating. How often people make harsh judgments based solely on their perception of a person's life events and choices. All I wanted as a young woman was to be treated with the same privileges as my brother, and as a result, I was raped. A part of me held on to the belief that I was somehow responsible for what happened to me. For years, the sight of that dimly lit neon-green clock on my parents' stove made me nauseous. I associated sex with rape and could not see the appeal in intimacy.

I'd never told Jason about the rape; I had wanted to wipe away the memory. I chose to be intimate with him early on in our courtship, hoping it could erase the violence I had been subjected to. I thought that if I had sex on my own terms, I might regain some sense of control over my body. He assumed I was a virgin. I was afraid that if he knew the truth, he would be turned off and see me as flawed, dirtied or sullied. He might think that I wasn't wholesome and therefore deserving of his love. In putting that experience in a box buried deep within me, I never allowed myself to heal. I never found sex pleasurable. Intercourse always led me back to that moment of violation frozen within me. The few times I tried to relax and enjoy the intimacy, I felt immense guilt. I thought that if I allowed myself to explore and relish my sexuality, I was telling the girl on that sofa-bed that what she went through didn't matter.

It took a mental breakdown for me to finally deal with this experience and start trusting that there can be pleasure and passion when it comes to sex.

When Dustin came into my life, I was shedding layers of myself that weren't serving me. I was done with guilt, fear, worry and limiting beliefs. I wanted to experience passion, both physical and emotional. I was upfront with him about my first sexual experience, and as we became physically intimate, I realized that healing these wounds would be the only way I could move forward. I couldn't continue to pretend that it never happened or that I was responsible for it. Over the years, the pain has gently dislodged itself from my body. But some of it still remains and always will. The trauma I suffered eroded my trust, my sense of self, and so much more. It may never go away completely, but identifying it, giving it a name and holding it to the light has helped with my healing.

...

Sitting on that bathroom floor, holding my head in my hands, I sobbed, finding myself, once again, violated by someone who claimed to care about me. Jason had no right to see me naked and vulnerable anymore. I felt sick. I didn't want him to know about Dustin. I wasn't leaving him for Dustin. I was leaving because our relationship was over and had been for a long time. And, now that he knew that there was someone else, he would never accept that I ended our marriage because I no longer loved him. He hadn't wanted to accept it from the start; why would he now? He had the perfect reason to explain why I was leaving: I was in love with someone else.

Jason signed the separation papers and changed the title of the house to his name shortly after he confronted me about Dustin. I was relieved that we finally seemed to be moving forward on the separation.

But then he slowly started taking up more space in the house. After years of insisting that he had no option but to work evening shifts, he was suddenly working days. He had let me do the majority of the heavy lifting and caring for the kids since they were born, but now he insisted on driving them to school and daycare every morning. At the time, this didn't trigger alarm bells, but in hindsight, I can see he was asserting his dominance, reinforcing himself as the 'parent who stayed.'

One day, on my way to work, Aidan's school called to ask if he would be absent all day. I informed the secretary that Jason was driving him in. I suggested that she call him to see if perhaps Aidan wasn't feeling well. I called the daycare to find that Cassie still hadn't shown up. I felt a pit in the bottom of my stomach. Once I got to the office, I called the house and Jason's mom answered the phone. She put him on and he told me that he had decided to take the day off and keep the kids with him. 'Quality time,' he'd said. I hung up feeling anxious.

I left work early and parked on the street in front of the house. Walking up the driveway, I could see Cassie in the window. I waved to her and she shyly waved back. I watched as Jason's mom took her by the hand and led her away from the window. And in that moment, everything around me slowed down. I put my key in the lock and instinctively knew it wouldn't work. I could see Aidan standing at the top of the stairs through the frosted windowpane. I felt the panic rising in my throat and my thoughts circling. Why did he take the day off? Why did he keep the kids home with him?

It all came together when I rang the doorbell and watched him walk up the stairs from the basement. He was holding a black garbage bag, and when he opened the door he had a sneer on his face. He stood in the doorway, blocking me.

'Why isn't my key working?' I asked, trying to push past him.

'I changed the locks.'

'What? Why would you change the locks?'

He stretched his arm across the doorway. 'Because, as of last night, this is my house.' He seemed pleased with himself.

'Jason, don't do this. Please,' I pleaded. I looked past him at Aidan holding onto the baby gate at the top of the stairs. 'You don't have to do this. They won't understand. We have a calendar. They know that I'm moving out at the end of the month.' My eyes watered, a lump forming in my throat.

'I don't fucking care about your calendar,' he hissed, his face close to mine. He dropped the garbage bag on the stoop. 'Here's your shit. You can get the rest of it at the end of the month. Now, get off my property.'

Aidan pushed and pulled at the baby-gate, trying to open it. The lump in my throat was getting bigger. I looked over Jason's shoulder at my scared little boy and tried to smile.

'It's okay, Aidan. Don't cry, kiddo. It's okay,' I said, choking back tears.

I noticed Cassie wriggling in her grandmother's arms by the bedrooms. She squirmed out and ran to the gate. They both stood there, crying. I wanted to push him out of the way, run up the stairs and take them with me.

He turned to them and said softly, 'It's okay, guys, Daddy's right here.' With his hand on the door, he gave me a wicked smile. 'Oh, and by the way, your perfect little world is about to come crashing down.'

He slammed the door shut and locked it. I stood, paralyzed, and watched him slowly walk up the stairs and open the baby gate. He put his arms around the kids and hugged them tightly.

•••

I blinked and looked around. I picked up the garbage bag without opening it, slowly walked to my car and put it in the trunk. I climbed into the driver's seat and my phone rang.

'Hello?' I answered, still stunned.

'Babe, it's me. Where are you?'

'I'm at the house. Jason changed the locks. I don't know what to do. I don't—'

'He called my wife.'

'What? How?' I looked up and saw Jason standing by the front window, arms crossed over his chest, smiling. 'That's what he meant,' I whispered.

'What are you talking about?'

'He said that my perfect little world was about to come crashing down.' I closed my eyes. 'What are you going to do?' I asked Dustin.

'I guess I'll go home and face the music.'

I looked up at the window again and watched Jason close the blinds. I started the car and drove a few blocks before pulling over and turning off the engine. Gripping the steering wheel, I could feel the tears pouring down my face. Images, conversations and moments Dustin and I had shared over the last two years played through my mind. I was mentally exhausted. I was emotionally drained from the past four months of sharing a house with Jason after telling him I wanted a divorce. I couldn't imagine what Dustin's wife must have felt when she learned that her husband was being unfaithful.

I sent Jason a furious text, telling him that he had no right to call her. He responded that he felt it was his duty to let her know what her husband had done. I threw the phone to the backseat. I was convinced Jason had called her as a way of punishing me. He wanted me to feel pain, the same heartache he did. I was certain he was hoping that Dustin would put an end to our relationship and mend his marriage.

And yet, as scared, sad and angry as I was, a part of me was relieved that Dustin's wife knew about us. I told myself that this could be the end of living a double life. In the past year, we had often imagined having a future together.

Maybe now we could have the life we both wanted.

The Aftermath

Jason and I were now officially separated. Dustin's wife knew about us. Everything was out in the open. She insisted they attend couple's therapy, and Dustin agreed. He thought this could bring closure for them—that through therapy, she would also realize that their marriage was over.

He was attending a conference in Toronto and asked if I would spend the weekend with him. As soon as I caught a glimpse of him in the dense crowd at the train station, I knew he was going to end our relationship. I considered turning around and getting back on the train. Instead, I decided to stay and spend this last bit of time with the man I loved. That weekend, we agreed that while he was in couple's therapy, we would not communicate. I was heartbroken, but I wanted him to figure out his situation without me in the way.

We spent the next two days ignoring the fact that these moments might be our last. When we made love, there was a passionate sorrow to it. We held each other and cried. He left after I fell into a deep, exhausted sleep. Before leaving the hotel room, I found a note taped to the bathroom mirror. 'I will <u>always</u> love you.' I still have that note in a box, with all of the cards and letters he wrote me.

Three months passed, and we kept our promise of no communication. I figured that they had decided to work through their marital issues. So, I focused on myself, my kids and my work. I still longed to hear from him, hoping he would show up at my apartment and tell me he loved me and wanted to be with me.

Jason enjoyed taunting me about the fact that my perfect plan hadn't worked out. He offered his forgiveness. 'You could come back home. We could give the kids what they deserve—two parents under the same roof.'

These were challenging months. He would flip back and forth between angry and bitter and sad and forgiving. I could not understand how he could still think that there was any chance of a reconciliation. Why would he want to be with someone who didn't love him? After all the pain and anguish we had put each other through, why would he think I would even consider giving our failed marriage another chance? Why would I subject myself to the mental agony that would inevitably be attached to me for ending our union? I knew that I would never be forgiven for my perceived sins, but I hoped that we would eventually be able to respectfully co-parent our children.

Although Dustin was no longer in my life, I did not question my decision to end my marriage. His absence reinforced that leaving Jason was the right choice. I was happier outside of my marriage than in it, and I found comfort knowing that, though I'd paid such a high price for it, I was better off on my own.

One sunny Saturday afternoon, I was making hot chocolate for the kids after playing at the park for an hour. While they were flipping through the cartoon channels, I heard my phone ping. It was a message from Dustin. I froze. *I still love you. And I miss you.*

I put the phone back in my purse without responding. I wasn't going to get sucked back into our relationship as it had been. If he was still in therapy with his wife, I didn't want to be involved. Of course, that night, lying in bed, I ran through all the possible scenarios in my mind. The next day, he emailed me. Therapy wasn't working. He wanted a divorce. He just needed to tell her. He didn't know how to. He hated hurting his family. Again, I didn't respond.

Two days later, he called me at the office to say that he had accepted an eighteen-month secondment working directly with the Commissioner of the Canadian Tax Authority. Hearing his voice made my heart ache. 'Congratulations. That's a big job. I'm happy for you.'

'The position is in Ottawa,' he continued.

'Oh. Are you moving the whole family?' I asked, trying to sound flippant.

'No, it's just me.'

I held my breath. 'Does that mean …'

'It means that they are staying in Calgary.'

I told myself that if he was moving on his own for such a long time, surely it had to mean that his marriage was over. I thought that maybe this would be a first step in their separation. His move date was set, and he flew into town on a weekend when I didn't have the kids.

My heart was fluttering as I waited for him at the airport arrivals. I didn't know what to expect. We hadn't seen each other for months. I could barely hold back the tears when his eyes met mine. He walked briskly down the stairs, never breaking eye contact, and pulled me in close when he reached me. He kissed my face and wiped the tears from my cheeks. We held each other tightly and whispered how much we'd missed one another. The rest of the world fell away as I breathed him in. When we finally broke loose from our embrace, his suitcase was the only one going around the baggage carousel. We held hands and walked to my car in silence. My world felt whole again. *Our* world felt whole again.

We looked at three apartments, and Dustin signed a lease. At the airport, he took off his watch and handed it to me. 'I want you to keep this,' he said. 'It's not a ring, but it's a promise that I'll be back soon.'

I laughed. 'I guess we're going steady now.'

A few weeks later, I picked him up from the airport again. We drove to his apartment and unpacked his things. He had given me a key when he signed the lease and I had stocked the fridge and pantry. We prepared dinner together, dancing to hip-hop in the kitchen, laughing. When we held each other in bed that night, he suggested that I bring some of my things over to his apartment so that I wouldn't need to pack a bag when staying over. I fell asleep feeling carefree and filled with hope that we would always be this happy. I finally had someone in my corner who could help me navigate my messy divorce.

For the first three years after we separated, Jason and I shared custody of the kids with hand-offs on Fridays. While most people love Fridays, I grew to hate them. I could always count on the same unpleasant and emotional conversations on those nights.

'Mommy, why did you break the family?' Aidan would ask on the drive home. He needed to get the words out of his system right away.

I would take a deep breath and say, 'Mommy didn't break the family, Aidan. We are still a family, just a different one now.'

'No. You left us. And you left Daddy and you broke our family. You're not in our family anymore.'

My hands would tighten around the steering wheel. *Keep your tone light.* I'd look at him in the rearview mirror and smile.

'Aidan, Mommy did not leave you and Cassie. Mommy and Daddy were not happy and that's why we are not living together anymore. It doesn't change the fact that we are still and always will be a family. Mommy and Daddy love you and Cassie very much.'

Quiet. I could almost hear him thinking. 'Daddy says that you broke the family and that you left us.'

Deep breaths. *Tread lightly*, I'd remind myself, *don't put them in the middle of this.*

'Honey, I'm sorry that you think that I broke the family. But I will always be your mommy, and that means that we will always be a family. You, me and Cassie are a family. Daddy is your family. Mami and Papi are your family, and so are Granny and Grandad. They don't all live with you, do they? And your aunts, uncles and cousins? Aren't they all part of your family?'

He'd look out the window. I could see his little jaw clenching in the rearview mirror. *Thinking, he's thinking.* He'd bite his lower lip. 'Yeah, I guess.' Sigh of relief. Crisis averted, until next week.

I refused to play the blame game. I was careful not to say anything unkind about Jason around the kids. I would listen, empathize, hug and try to calm them down. At the end of the night we would usually all fall into one bed, read stories and go to sleep together. Once they were sound asleep, I would move them to their own beds and tuck them in. I would then make my way back to my own room and cry—for the loss of their innocence, the unnecessary pain they were suffering, and myself.

Every time, I would pray for the strength to continue staying above spitefulness and protecting them from this divorce poison. I would call Dustin and recount my evenings. He would comfort me, saying I was being a good mother for not allowing my anger and resentment to cloud my judgment.

Over time, we came up with a plan about how to introduce him to them. One evening, I was sitting at the kitchen table drawing with the kids when the doorbell rang. Cassie looked up at me, frowning.

'Who dat?' she asked.

'It's Mommy's special friend. Remember, I told you guys he would stop by to say hello?' I said, walking to the door.

Dustin planted a quick kiss on my cheek coming through the doorway. Aidan and Cassie were focused on their drawings. He gave my shoulder a reassuring squeeze.

'Guys, this is DJ. DJ, that's Aidan, and this is Cassie.'

'Hi, DJ,' Aidan said without looking up.

'Hi, Aidan, it's nice to meet you,' Dustin said, extending his hand. Aidan stood up and shook it vigorously, a shy smile on his face.

Cassie looked up at him, a mischievous glint in her eyes. 'Do you want to dwaw with me?' she asked, her lisp noticeable. It had gotten worse since the separation.

'Sure, I'd love to,' he said, taking off his suit jacket. He sat next to her and winked at me.

'So, DJ, where do you live?' Aidan asked, sizing him up. 'And why are you wearing a fancy suit?'

'I have to wear this fancy suit for work, but I don't really like it. It's too hot,' he said, undoing a shirt button and pulling at the collar, sticking his tongue out. Aidan laughed and continued with this interrogation.

I poured us each a glass of Chardonnay. Handing one to Dustin, I saw that while he had been talking to Aidan, Cassie had drawn on the cuff of his shirt with her markers.

'Cassie, why did you draw on DJ's shirt?' I asked, embarrassed.

She looked at me sheepishly, her lower lip quivering. 'Hey, it's okay, don't worry about it. I'm sure it'll wash right out,' Dustin reassured her.

She wiped her eyes and looked up at him with a big grin. 'Do you wanna see my play house?' she asked, pointing to the large cardboard box in the living room. They both led him into it, and he peered out of the big cut-out windows and waved to me.

'Come out, DJ, I want to show you something.'

My eyes widened as I watched Aidan take one of the cardboard shutters off and smack him in the chest with it. Cassie giggled and jumped on his back. Dustin laughed and started chasing them around the house. I smiled and placed a hand on my heart. Dustin was right, it would be okay. He'd be DJ, Mommy's special friend. DJ, the nickname his own father had given him as a child.

The kids had been told time and again that a bad man named Dustin broke our family and stole Mommy away. Now they would be able to get to know DJ and decide for themselves how they felt about him. By the time Jason figured out that DJ and Dustin were one and the same, it would be too late to convince them that he was the bad man.

With Dustin by my side, I was able to relax and not worry so much about when Jason might strike next. His calmness grounded me when I'd get worked up over a text or email I'd received from Jason. He reminded me often that I didn't always have to fight back. 'The kids are here with us; everything is fine, babe. Turn your phone off,' he'd say.

He'd repeat these words often over the years. He'd remind me that sometimes the best thing to do is nothing. 'He can only hurt you if you allow him in.'

As happy as we were during his assignment, his expected return to Calgary weighed heavily. Neither of us wanted to talk about what this would mean for us. While he and his wife had been living apart for over a year, they were not officially separated. He would periodically commute to Calgary and always assured me that he was spending all of his time with his daughter. I wanted to believe him, but I knew that he was also spending time with his wife. While I was torn apart by this reality, I hoped that the moments they shared were spent discussing their inevitable separation.

My friends continually reminded me that I deserved better than a part-time relationship with a married man and to be with someone who would give all of himself to me. I knew they were right, but my love for Dustin ran too deep. He was in my veins, and I could not imagine a life without him in it. I did not want to imagine a life without him in it. The defining moment came when his secondment ended. 'So, what now?' I asked.

'Sonia, please. I'm with you. I love you.'

'Okay, so, what's the plan?'

His shoulders slumped and he sighed. 'I can't just tell her that I want a divorce as soon as I land.'

'You're right. You should have told her that before you took the assignment.' My words were sharp.

For as long as I have been with Dustin, I have been judged harshly for being in a relationship with a married man. Over the years I've been called a slut, a whore, and a home-wrecker. I've had women who don't know me personally tell me that they don't like my 'type.' These are strangers, who have formed an opinion of me and labelled me as a bad person without even knowing our story. And I get it. It is unforgivable to fall in love with some-one else's spouse. My life would have been a lot easier had Dustin not been married. But what frustrates me and makes me livid is that Dustin hasn't had to face this type of judgment. There is only one villain here—and that is me, as if I am one hundred percent responsible for fifty percent of a rela-tionship, the same way I am blamed for the breakdown of my marriage with Jason. The fault falls exclusively on my shoulders.

Now that I have experience of them, I know that affairs are not exclusive to the bedroom. One-night stands are. In my opinion, affairs begin when one half of a couple starts looking outside the marriage for something that is missing in their marriage. The first two years that Dustin and I were having an affair, we lived over three thousand kilometers apart, with a two-hour time difference. We spent most of this time developing an emotional rela-tionship. We wrote letters, talked on the phone several times a day, emailed, texted and Skyped as often as we could. When he was in town for work, we spent as much time as we could together. We made love every chance we had. We held each other, my head on his chest, fingers intertwined, planning our future together. The deep connection we developed is the reason we are still together. The compatibility in the bedroom was an added bonus. I'm not proud of the way Dustin and I met, knowing that so many people were hurt in the process of us coming together. If I could have chosen differently, I would have.

After all the pain and hurt I had suffered, I was desperate to feel something good in my life—something unrelated to my kids and the love and joy they brought me. I wanted someone to look at me as though I was special; as though I was funny and intelligent and beautiful. I wanted to feel sexy and desirable. Dustin made me feel all of these things, and so much more. With him, I could just be me without pretense, faking, or pretending. He gave me everything I wanted in a relationship, and I did the same for him.

Now that we have been living together for eleven years, I can look at our relationship and see that it is not a neatly packaged love story with birds chirping and a horse-drawn carriage. It's ugly and messy, and we left a bloody trail.

But how we came to be together doesn't change the fact that our love is real, that it was real from the beginning.

Co-parenting Anxiety

All my life, I have felt things deeply. I become overwhelmed when I am out of my element. The anxiety I'd lived with since I was a child ramped up after I moved out of the marital home. I had never lived by myself before. I'd lived with my parents, then with roommates, and lastly, Jason, the boyfriend who became my husband.

Nothing could have prepared me for the quietness of an empty home without my children in it. I would turn the TV on, trying to drown out the voices in my head questioning my decisions. I counted the minutes until the kids were back to fill the place with life. I preferred tantrums over silence. I quickly got used to Jason ringing the doorbell in the evenings after the kids had gone to bed. He'd leave packages on my doorstep. Photos with angry messages, candlesticks from our wedding day, personal items that he'd kept hidden from me. His behavior verged on stalking and harassment, and it frightened me—it was difficult for me to see that he was grieving.

We were still unable to talk to each other face to face. I had stopped responding to the letters and emails and was overwhelmed with the rapid-fire text messages every night when the kids were with me. To make things worse, my relationship with Aidan was suffering. We were struggling to connect. He seemed angry all the time. He would throw tantrums, punch, kick and lash out. I talked to Jason, and he dismissed me, saying there were no issues at his house, suggesting that perhaps I was the problem.

When I asked our family doctor to refer us to a child psychiatrist, Jason instead offered that he and I seek counselling. To help us transition into this new 'co-parenting relationship,' although he didn't use those words. I agreed, believing that his willingness to discuss the issues with a therapist was progress.

I sat in the waiting room at the therapist's office. I looked at my watch, thinking that he was going to be a no-show, when he walked in. 'Hi,' I said, almost too eager.

He glared at me stone-faced and sat down.

The office door opened and the therapist invited us in. He shook her hand, smiling, and introduced himself. My anxiety was already high, and my throat felt tight as I stood. Her office was quaint. There was a desk, three chairs, a small sofa and a coffee table. I took a seat on the sofa and immediately regretted my foolish choice. Jason sat on the chair at the opposite end of the room. I wondered why I'd needed all this space. Was I expecting him to sit next to me in a gesture of unity, in our desire to co-parent kindly and efficiently? He couldn't even respond to a simple hello; why the hell would he sit next to me?

Before she even had a chance to begin, he explained that he didn't agree with therapy; in his opinion, we had no issues co-parenting, and if I was having problems with the kids, I should either let him deal with them or figure it out on my own.

'If you feel so strongly, why are you here?' she asked him softly.

'Because I don't want my son to have to see a child psychiatrist. And if I'm going to do this, she had better start being honest,' he said, pointing to me.

The therapist leaned back in her chair and looked at me. 'Sonia, will you be honest in these sessions?'

'Of course.' I turned to him. 'When have I not been honest? I'm the one who keeps coming to you with the issues I'm having when the kids are with me. I'm trying to make sure that you're involved and that I'm not keeping things from you.'

'Oh really?' he asked sitting forward in his chair. 'How about when you were sleeping with someone else and lying about it? We both know what a good liar you are, so maybe that's why I don't believe you when you say there are issues with Aidan. He's perfectly fine when he's with me.'

I felt like I'd been punched in the gut. This was a trap. I hung my head, sensing the therapist's eyes on me. I bit the inside of my lip to stop the tears from coming.

'Sonia, I think that before we move on to the co-parenting issues, we need to address the trust issues. Perhaps we need to give Jason a chance to speak his mind and get things off his chest so we can move forward with a clean slate.' She looked over at him and he nodded. 'Are you willing to be honest with him about anything he asks you while we are here? I think this will help to start to rebuild some of the trust.'

I turned back to Jason. 'Look, I'm sorry. I am sorry that I cheated on you. I shouldn't have. It wasn't okay, and I'm sorry.' I moved forward on the sofa, trying to get him to look at me. 'I wasn't happy. We weren't happy. Our marriage was broken long before I slept with another guy. I was lonely. I … I wanted to feel wanted. I shouldn't have done it, but I can't change what I did.' I clasped my hands. 'Can we please, please, move past this and try to co-parent our kids?'

He crossed his arms over his chest. 'Like I've told you before, I have no issues with Aidan when he's with me. He has no tantrums, he shows no aggression, in fact he's a very happy little boy.'

I sighed. 'Okay, but we can't just ignore how much his behavior changes when he's with me. I think that we should sit down with him together and talk to him. Figure out what's going on in his head. No?'

The therapist looked at Jason. 'Are you willing to do what Sonia is asking? Perhaps it could help if you both talked to him together. It will give you both a better understanding of his behavior with the other parent. He might feel more comfortable to share his feelings if he's in the presence of both his parents.'

He shook his head. 'No. It'll only confuse them more if we start to do things together. They are still struggling to accept that their mother has left us; I don't want to have them think that we could be a family again.' He turned to me. 'If you really are having issues with Aidan, you should just let me deal with it. I'll talk to him and tell him that he needs to behave properly when he's at your house, just like he does when he's at home.'

I shook my head. 'IF he has issues? Wow, you really don't believe me, do you?'

'What can I say? I find it hard to see the truth through all of your lies. All I'm saying is that my son is happy when he's home. So if he's not happy when he's with you, you might want to look in the mirror and see where the problem really is.' He clenched his jaw, looking away from me. I followed his gaze to the clock sitting on the therapist's desk. 'Our time is up. You can pay for this one,' he said, standing up. He grabbed his jacket and left the door open behind him.

I reached into my purse with shaky hands and pulled out my checkbook. I wiped the tears off my cheeks with the back of my hand. 'Do I make it out to you directly?' I asked.

She nodded and leaned forward to put a hand on my knee. 'You are very brave.'

We went to a few more joint sessions, but no good came from them. Jason didn't believe we had any difficulties co-parenting. He continued to repeat that, if there were issues with the kids, the solution was to let him deal with it. As much as I wanted us to be united in our approach, he continued to say that it would only confuse the kids if we talked to them together. We were no longer a family and we shouldn't give them any hope of a reconciliation by showing a unified front. At the time, I didn't understand his reasoning. Looking back, I realize that maybe it was just too painful for him to be around me.

I continued to see the therapist on my own. Her advice was invaluable in getting Aidan's outbursts under control. She offered unwavering support, and the neutrality she brought in her suggestions kept me sane. I continued to see her for three years. My last session was a few days before I moved to Calgary. Once again, she leaned forward, touched my knee and said, 'You are very brave.'

These small acts of kindness kept me going through the darkest hours.

The Arena

Aidan's hockey was always a challenge for me. I had no idea how to properly put on his equipment and I could never tie his skates tight enough. The therapist had suggested it might be less distracting for him if only one parent took him to the rink at a time. This might minimize the stress he felt of having to 'pick a side.' Because we had a one-week-on, one-week-off custody arrangement, this was easily doable. However, Jason didn't care much for the therapist's suggestions. He and his family came to every game, practice and tournament. I could only control what I did on my weeks and chose to follow the therapist's advice not to attend events outside of my time with the kids. Unfortunately, when Aidan and I became alienated later on, my not attending every game and practice was used to fan the flames and was interpreted as me displaying a 'lack of support.'

I looked at the clock: 5:30 a.m. Who schedules five-year-olds' hockey practice for 6:30 on a Saturday morning? I yawned, stretched and looked at the clock again: 5:32 a.m. 'This is ridiculous,' I mumbled, kicking off the blankets.

I opened Aidan's door and looked at him sleeping soundly, his eyelashes long and dark against his cheeks. I knelt by his bed, gently pulling his blanket down from his chin.

'Time to wake up, A,' I said, rubbing his chubby cheek. 'You've got to eat something before your practice.'

'I'm tired, Mommy,' he said, eyes still closed. I considered letting him sleep. But the last time I had decided to let him miss his practice, I never heard the end of it. I was bombarded with messages all weekend, and I couldn't face that again.

'Come on, kiddo. You'll be fine once you wake up,' I said, turning his bedroom light on.

I walked into Cassie's room. 'Good morning, sweet girl, time to get up. We don't want to be late for Aidan's practice.'

'Noooooo, I don't wanna get up,' she whined, turning away, pulling the blankets up over her head. 'I'll buy you a hot chocolate on the way to the arena,' I tried bribing her.

They sat at the kitchen table, eyes half opened, eating. 'Mommy, do I have to go to practice?' Aidan asked as I laid out his equipment.

'Yeah, kiddo, you do. You can't miss every time you're with me. It's important that you go and learn your skills with the other kids.' I walked over and kissed the top of his head. Pulling his chin up, I gave him my biggest smile. 'Besides, once you get there, you'll have so much fun.'

I looked at the clock on the oven: 5:57 a.m. *Shit*. I was supposed to be at the arena at 6 a.m. No time to stop for a hot chocolate. I hurried the kids and we pulled into the parking lot at 6:12 a.m.

I was standing on Cassie's side of the car, leaning on Aidan's hockey stick with his equipment bag over my shoulder, trying to convince her to get out. One of the other parents walked by and offered to take Aidan in for me.

'Come on, Cassie, you gotta help me here,' I begged as she folded her arms over her chest, pouting. 'Mommy can't carry you in, honey, I'm already carrying Aidan's heavy bag and my hands are full.'

'Daddyyyyyy!' she shrieked, looking over my shoulder. Jumping out of her seat, she pushed past me. I braced myself and turned around.

Cassie jumped up into his arms. 'Hi, my princess, I missed you,' he said, kissing her face. 'You're late,' he growled, looking at me.

'I'm here,' I responded, trying to stay calm. I grabbed my hat and gloves and closed the car door. 'Can you please put her down; she can walk into the arena. She doesn't have to be carried all the time.'

'I don't mind carrying her, right, princess?' he said, hugging her even tighter. She giggled as he tickled her over her coat. I closed my eyes and let out a deep sigh. Walking into the arena with Cassie in his arms, he let the door close on me. I wrestled with the hockey bag, my purse, hat and gloves. Clenching my jaw, I pushed opened the door and saw his parents talking to Cassie. *Don't these people sleep in on weekends?* I wondered.

'Cassie, come with Mommy, please. I have to go finish getting Aidan ready. Come on,' I said, grabbing at her hand.

'Mommyyyyyyy, no. I want to stay with Daddy and Granny and Grandad,' she screamed, pulling away. It wasn't worth creating a scene if I forced her to come with me.

In the locker room, I helped Aidan put on his skates, jersey, helmet and gloves. 'Alright, kiddo, time to go on the ice. I'll be sitting at the top with your sister,' I said, hurrying him out.

I pushed him along with the other kids and looked around to see where Cassie was. I put my hat and gloves on, rubbing my hands together. I spotted her at the other end of the rink, sitting with Jason and his parents. She looked over and I waved. She waved back with a big grin. I motioned for her to come and sit with me, and she shook her head no. I watched as she brought the hot chocolate cup up to her lips, and my heart sank. No chance she would sit with me now.

There was always an ache in my belly when I saw Jason's mother at the arena. I had to hold back from running over and wrapping my arms around her. I loved her deeply. I had spent so much time with her over the years, and I thought of her as a second mother. As a mother myself, I completely understood that her loyalty remained with her son and that she could not betray him by maintaining a relationship with me. But knowing this did nothing to diminish the wave of sadness I felt whenever she avoided my gaze, or worse, looked at me with such contempt. Aidan was her first grandchild, and she adored him. And then Cassie came along, the first granddaughter, a perfect little doll. Looking longingly over at her, I remembered having tea one afternoon as the kids played at our feet in the living room, and how I opened up to her about the issues Jason and I were having. She had listened, sympathetically nodding. When I asked for her advice, she'd said, 'Stay. For the kids. You have to make it work. They need two parents under the same roof.'

In the early years of my marriage to Jason, his cousin and wife separated. They shared custody of their young son. I remember how torn the entire family was over this divorce. We attended a birthday party for their son the year after they split up, and I was amazed to see how cordial the parents and both sets of grandparents were to one another. Seeing this firsthand gave me confidence that Jason and I would be able to be respectful co-parents and that both sets of grandparents might also help create a peaceful environment for their grandkids. This wasn't the case. My decision to end my marriage turned me into the enemy. Being the mother of their grandchildren did not earn me any kindness or respect from Jason's parents. All the love and inclusivity I was shown during my eleven-year relationship with their son vanished overnight. I didn't expect we would remain close. But I also didn't expect our relationship to become so bitter. Once again, I found myself isolated, an outsider. Like too many times before, I was locked out, an outcast desperately looking through the glass, trying to find a way in.

The hockey arena became a place of anxiety and frustration, where I felt bullied. I often wonder if that's why I've struggled to be supportive of Aidan's passion for the game. I dreaded the encounters with Jason's family, the side-eye, the constant push and pull of the kids. I didn't want to join in this game of emotional bribery and shows of loyalty, where the kids had to choose between their parents. Instead, I lost out on my time with them. The only time the arena felt safe was when Dustin was with me. My in-laws stayed away when he was by my side.

I started to feel suffocated in this small town, where Jason and his family had always lived. I continually worried about running into them at restaurants, coffee shops or the grocery store. In their presence, I felt constantly judged and belittled. I knew I could not continue to live in such close proximity if I wanted to stay sane. I didn't want Jason to be able to show up on my doorstep whenever he pleased or to criticize everything I did or did not do, during my weeks with the kids. I wanted my freedom. I needed some peace.

So when Dustin and I started planning the next phase of our relationship, I was ready to pack up and leave this town. My health and well-being depended on it.

Mommy Always Leaves

As time went by, the kids always seemed bitter and angry with me. I knew it was hard for them to be around me and their dad at the same time. I could see it in their body language—the way they cowered, avoiding eye contact, almost as if by looking at the ground, they didn't have to pick a side.

We did the hand-offs at the daycare and then later at school, to minimize the interactions. I preferred it that way. Seeing Jason was too much for me. I never knew which Jason I would have to face—the sad one or the angry one. Much as I hate to admit it, I preferred the angry one, because at least I could resent him. When it was the sad one, I felt terrible—not because I still loved him or thought there was a chance of a reconciliation but because I could see the pain I had caused him. It was etched into his raw vulnerability, which he'd seldom showed me while we were married. Luckily, he would not stay sad for very long. He also seemed to prefer the angry version of himself.

Telling him I wanted a divorce had been like lighting the match after dousing our lives with gasoline. He made it seem as if I had walked away unscathed from a burning house, leaving everything in ashes. Looking back, of course I see the damage I caused. It wasn't just my house I burnt down, it was his too. And my kids'. It all went up in flames, and I did not know what parts would survive the raging fire. Was the structure solid enough for us to co-parent, like decent human beings? Would we be able to put our kids first and ourselves last? I believe I tried as best I could, but it wasn't all up to me. It was a two-person job. Jason stayed smothered in smoke and ashes for years. He kept the kids covered in ash so that they could all be broken together. I suppose this was his way of ensuring that everyone would remember who'd started the fire, without understanding that I had walked away with burns of my own.

For years, he played the wounded and broken man whose wife had wronged him. He insisted that all the love he had to give should go to his children, not recognizing what a burden this would place on them. We tried therapy, mediation—nothing worked. We were different people at different places in our lives, and neither of us wanted to budge. Neither of us wanted to put aside these differences and accept our part in the breaking of our vows. Neither of us was able to put the kids first. He clung to his victimhood as steadfastly as I did to mine. He was a victim of my adultery, and I was a victim of his alienation. We were so busy vying for the role of the bigger victim, we never came to terms with the fact that our children were the real casualties in this whole situation.

They were too young to be thrown into the middle of the hate-storm that was wrecking their lives. I don't know if it makes me a terrible mother that I chose to move to another city. Perhaps it does. That decision was the hardest one of my life, by far. I had spent a lifetime putting others first, sharing everything that was special to me. I lived in extremes, from having my virginity stolen from me to being slut-shamed for being with a married man. I'd been chastised for refusing to stay in an unhappy marriage for my children's sake, only to find myself continually pushing against parental alienation. And so I made the decision to do what was best for me. I chose to put my needs first—a behavior I had been taught to believe was wrong. It continues to be held against me to this day.

But I'm not alone. Women have been taught that our needs should always come last. From birth, we are shaped to believe that our identity consists of what we mean to others. We are daughters, sisters, wives, mothers. These labels imply that we must be selfless; that we exist to be of service to others. But I've learned through the years that if I don't put myself first and allow time for self-care, whatever that looks like at any given moment, I am not the best version of myself. These days I remind my daughter that putting herself and her needs first is not selfish—it's healthy self-interest. It's what a person who considers herself to be as important as those around her does.

By this stage, Dustin had separated from his wife, and we were ready to have a life together. We decided that it would be best if we lived in Calgary. He was already well established at his place of work, and I wanted to put some distance between me and Jason.

We had a meeting with a law firm in early January 2010 to discuss our options. The way they summed up our situation did not leave me hopeful.

The kids and I had been living in Glengarry since their birth. Jason still lived there, as well as their paternal grandparents, who were very involved in their lives when they were with their dad. Both kids were doing well at school, were involved in extracurricular activities and seemed well adjusted. They had a close and loving relationship with both parents and extended families. My parents lived a short distance away and were also intimately part of their lives.

Dustin had returned to Calgary when his assignment in Ottawa was done. We were not married, and therefore could not offer the classic 'stable family home' any better than Jason could. Moving to Calgary meant retiring from my job with the government; I would have to find work once I got there. And even though we had rented a three-bedroom apartment to ensure that the kids each had their own room, this apartment was in a new city and province, far from the familiar environment and the extended family they were used to.

•••

The odds were stacked against us. The lawyer explained that the Court would look at our petition for sole custody and permission to move them across the country and question why we would want to disrupt their seemingly peaceful life. Based on the firm's experience, we had a less than ten percent chance of being successful in court. The lawyer patted my hand and said, 'If I were you, I would take the exorbitant amount of money you will be spending on legal fees and use that to take your kids on nice trips.'

We agreed to reconvene the next morning. I got all the tears out of my system, coming to terms with the decision I was about to make. The next day, we devised our plan. I filed for full custody. It was important to make Jason believe I could win. He had to be worried enough to want to negotiate. I assumed I would get all the access and time I wanted if he was able to keep the kids in Glengarry. And that's how we proceeded. I texted him one evening as we were driving to an out-of-town hockey tournament with the kids.

'I'm moving to Calgary. I've filed for full custody of the kids. I've asked the Court to allow them to move with me. You'll be served by the bailiff tonight.'

As I expected, he wanted to negotiate.

Legalities aside, I was grappling with the fact that I had promised my son I wouldn't leave, and I was now breaking that promise. Over and over again, I had left. I had left when Jason changed the locks on the house we were still sharing. Standing at the top of the staircase crying, my children could not understand what was happening. All they'd seen was Mommy getting in her car and driving away, without a hug or a kiss or even a goodbye. For three years, every other Friday, I'd left them at daycare or school and said goodbye for another week. The time we'd spend together wasn't enough to replace the goodbyes. The leaving is what stuck in their minds.

I hoped that if we had enough time to process the changes that were coming, we could minimize some of the inevitable pain and sadness. But I could only control half of the narrative.

I prayed that having open and honest conversations with them would lessen the blow.

So I started talking to them about the move months before it was happening. I explained that nothing would change until school was over. And then, they would live with Daddy most of the school year. They would spend summer, spring break and Christmas holidays with Mommy. I would visit regularly in between. They were six and eight years old at the time. They never once asked if they could come with me. They wanted me to stay. They wanted everything to stay the same. But I didn't want that. I couldn't continue with the custody the way it was, and I couldn't handle co-parenting that closely with their father. I worried about the stories they would hear once I was gone. I wondered if the people I was leaving them with would be loving and compassionate when talking to them about their mother.

I was right to worry.

One-Way Ticket

I woke up the morning of June 20, 2010, with a heavy heart. The night before I was due to move, I took the kids out for one final dinner. Dropping them off at Jason's, I knelt on the front stoop of my old marital home—the same stoop where a garbage bag of my belongings had been dropped a few years earlier. I wrapped my arms around them both. I held them tightly, breathed them in, hoping their scent would never fade. Jason asked them to go inside and get ready for bed. I kissed their faces once more, squeezing their hands three times. *I. Love. You.* They waved from the living room window as I backed out of the driveway.

The drive to my parents' place was blurred by my tears as unending questions played on a loop in my head. Was I making a mistake? Should I stay? Should I have taken on a legal battle, even though the odds were stacked against us? Would the kids ever forgive me? Would they ever understand?

I pulled into the driveway and wiped my cheeks before walking into my parents' house, where I forced a smile. The air was heavy with unspoken words as we reminisced about my childhood. Everyone was careful not to say anything that might release an avalanche of feelings. The next day, they drove me to the airport. We ate one last lunch and they hugged me one more time before I got in line at the security gate. They stood and waited until I got through. I turned back to wave and saw my mom's face buried into Dad's chest, sobbing. He gave me a faint smile and nodded. I nodded back, swallowing the lump in my throat.

Making my way to the gate to board my plane with a one-way ticket to my new life, I looked around, wondering how many others were getting on a life-changing flight. The phone vibrated in my purse.

New message from DB: *Are you at the airport, babe?*

Yep. Just sitting at my gate.

New message from DB: *I'm headed into a meeting now. I can't wait to pick you up later and take you home. Our home.*

I looked at my watch. One hour before boarding. I sat facing the windows; the sun felt warm on my skin. I stared out at the row of planes. I sent Jason a text message. *Can I give the kids a quick call before I take off?*

I drummed my fingers on the table beside me. I took out the gossip magazine from my purse and flipped through it; the words and photos all blurred together. The flight crew walked through the doors. I sent Jason another text message. *I think I'll be boarding soon. If you get this within the next 15 minutes I'd like to call the kids.* I pressed send and watched the little envelope fly away.

I rubbed my temples, sighing. There was an announcement that boarding was about to begin. I waited, praying for a few more minutes. I boarded with the last group. Finding my seat, I pulled the cellphone out of my purse to turn it off. No new messages.

I closed my eyes as the plane took off, and my stomach tightened with excitement about what was to come and the pain of what I was leaving behind. Although I'd visited Dustin several times, I didn't know what to expect once I landed. I didn't have a job or know many people, and even though we had shared many months together in Ottawa during his executive assignment, we had never lived together in a real-life way.

In the time leading up to my move, I had visited Dustin often in Calgary, ensuring that I had met his teenagers and spent time with them prior to living there. We were slowly introduced and spent time together whenever I was in town. I made sure to give them the time and space they needed to get to know me. His daughter and I got on immediately, which helped with the transition of my move. Of course I knew that, like any blended family, we would have our share of bumps and bruises, but from the outset, they both could see how deeply I loved their dad.

I hoped that the love we had for each other would be enough to help us weather the storms that were to come.

Truth or Lie

I continued to feel judged, even by strangers, after I moved cities to be with Dustin. I'd struggle when people asked if I had children. Should I say yes and explain my decision to move without them? Or should I lie and say no? Either way, I always knew I was about to be judged harshly.

'I don't think I could ever leave my kids' usually marked the moment when I'd excuse myself from the conversation.

At a cocktail event for Dustin's employer, I met several of his peers for the first time. I was chatting with a friend, who asked about our plans for the Christmas break.

'I think we're going to take the kids to Banff for a few days. They've not seen the Rockies yet.'

A woman standing in the same circle approached us, extended her hand and introduced herself. 'I couldn't help but overhear you talking about your kids. How old are they?'

I hesitated. 'Aidan is nine and Cassie is seven.'

'Oh, that's a great age—mine are eight and ten, both boys. What school do they go to?'

I took a deep breath. 'You wouldn't be familiar with it. It's called Terre des Jeunes.'

'Is it a private school? I though the Lycée was the only French school in Calgary.'

'It's not in Calgary.' I bit the inside of my lower lip. 'They live with their dad in a small town in Ontario.'

'Oh. I, uh, I didn't realize that they aren't here with you.' There was an awkward pause and I shifted my weight from one foot to the other. 'I don't think that I could live without my kids.' She placed a hand on my arm. 'Do you miss them?'

I pulled away, tilted my head, raised one eyebrow and looked her square in the eyes. 'Oh God no, not one bit.'

What I really wanted to do was to slap this woman I had just met.

'If you'll excuse me,' I said and walked away. In the bathroom, I locked myself in a stall and sat with my face in my hands, tears streaming down my cheeks. When I opened the door, my friend was standing by the sink with her arms wide open, and I leaned in for a hug.

She rubbed my back and started laughing. 'The look on that woman's face was pure gold. I had to bite my cheek to not laugh in front of her.'

I pulled away and chuckled. 'It actually felt really good to be a bitch.'

'Screw these people,' she said, 'they don't know you and you don't owe them anything.'

I cannot count the times I have been asked why my kids aren't with me. How could I leave them behind, and move so far away from them? Why didn't I go to court? Was it a court decision, did I lose custody? I've spent years justifying myself to anyone and everyone who asks. It's as if people expect me to unpack all my past baggage to prove that I didn't abandon my children. I am always being forced to justify to loved ones and strangers alike that I actually do love my children—as if the enormity of my choice is lost on me. This wasn't some random coin toss, heads I fight, tails I don't. It was a carefully thought-out decision I have dissected a million times over the years. The thirty-four-year-old me made what she felt was the best decision at the time—the only one that could have saved me from a life of ongoing misery and despair.

So ask me if I miss my children at your peril. I dare you.

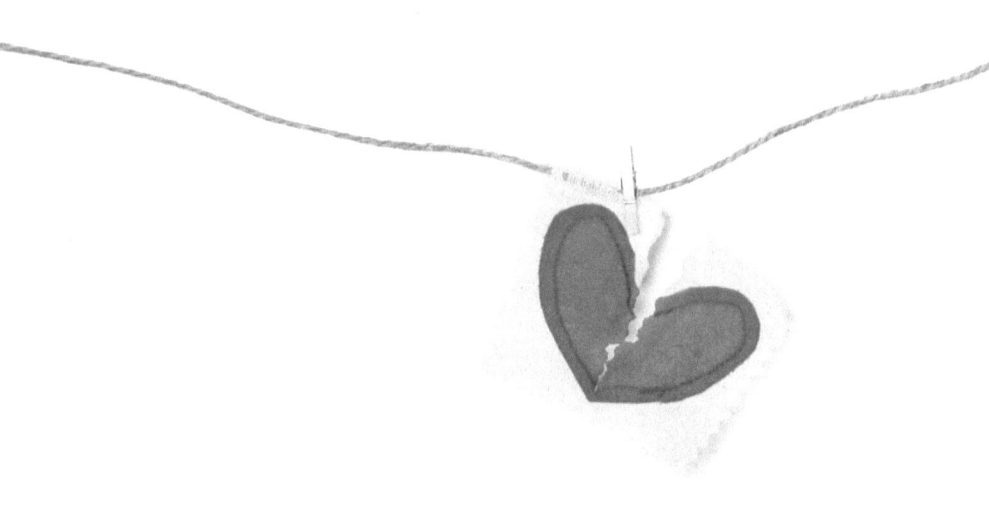

Turbulence

We were at the Calgary airport, standing at the arrivals gate. Throngs of people were streaming through the doors, falling into loved ones' arms. I paced nervously, hands clasped, waiting, anticipating. I looked around the thinning crowd. Their flight had landed forty-five minutes ago.

'Do you think they missed their flight?' I asked Dustin. I checked my phone to see if Jason had texted me. Nothing. 'Is that the flight crew?' I clenched my jaw. 'He's doing this on purpose, you know that, right? One last bit of control to piss me off before he hands them over for the summer.'

Dustin put his hands on my shoulders and squeezed. 'Breathe, honey. Doesn't matter if he's doing this on purpose. We're gonna have a great time with them.'

The doors opened and a few baggage handlers walked through. I could feel Dustin's eyes on me and tried to be cool. An airline employee pushed a passenger in a wheelchair. More people had started lining up at the arrivals for the next flights. When the doors closed, I saw a little face that I recognized. It was a split-second, but I was sure it was her.

They finally came out, one on each side of him, holding his hand. Cassie smiled at me coyly. Her hair was different. The long curls had been chopped chin length, with baby bangs.

'Here's their stuff,' Jason said, handing me a plastic grocery bag with a couple of half-empty water bottles, sweaters and some snacks. They each carried a small backpack. *Good thing I bought them clothes,* I thought, realizing he hadn't packed a suitcase.

He knelt and pulled them in. 'I'm going to miss you so, so much. Daddy is going to be so sad and lonely this summer. I don't even know what I'm going to do without you.'

I looked at Dustin over my shoulder and he tilted his head as if to say, 'Leave it alone.'

I took a step forward. 'Alright, guys. Give Daddy a big hug and say bye. We have to get going.'

He stood and pointed to me. 'I expect to speak to them whenever I want while they are with you.'

'I've never stopped you from speaking to them before, why would I now?' After one more hug, he made his way to the departures gate.

'Hi DJ,' Cassie said excitedly, wrapping her little arms around his waist. Aidan reached up to give him a high-five. Both kids gave Dustin their backpacks and slipped their small hands into mine. Walking to the parking lot, I asked, 'Hey, what happened to your hair, Cassie-bear?'

'It's 'cause I don't let Daddy brush it, so he said I have to cut it. But now it's short like yours, Mommy,' she said with a big grin.

'I think you look very pretty, Cassie, just like your Mom,' Dustin said.

'I got my hair cut too,' Aidan piped in, taking off his ballcap. His cowlick was more pronounced when his hair was short.

'Very nice,' I said, ruffling it. He smiled and his eyes softened.

I sat in the backseat with them, and a few minutes into the ride Aidan looked up at me, 'Mommy?'

'Yeah, kiddo?'

'You know you broke the family, eh?' Dustin's gaze caught mine in the rearview mirror. I blinked back the tears. 'Everyone hates you because you left us.' These words he had been holding on to, sitting at the back of his throat, had to be released. He pushed them out of his mouth as quickly he could. I was taken back to all of those Friday nights spent going around in circles about the divorce, the leaving, the broken family and all of the sadness. How it was all my fault. Always my fault.

I wondered how much of this they'd been hearing since I had moved away; how many stories had been spun. I resigned myself to being the villain, the liar, the cheater, the one who abandoned them, left them for a bad man named Dustin, the one-who-broke-the-family, who-broke-Daddy's-heart-and-now-he-will-never-be-the-same.

'Daddy is going to be all alone this summer and he's going to miss us,' he continued. 'You have DJ, but Daddy, he only has me and Cassie.'

I pulled him in closer and kissed the top of his head. 'It's okay, A, we can talk about all that when we get home.'

He leaned in and his body relaxed.

Long Goodbyes

The first summer the kids came to stay with us was easygoing. Dustin and I had agreed that I would start looking for work in the fall. He wanted me to be able to focus all my attention on enjoying my time with Aidan and Cassie. We spent our days roaming around the city, exploring the parks in the neighborhood and eating ice cream. We quickly fell into a routine, and, aside from the odd scuffle and sibling rivalry, the kids got along well.

Our summer ended far too quickly. I blinked and the day arrived for them to go back to their dad. Because they were so young, we had agreed we would accompany them ourselves on flights from one city to the other. While the round-trip in one day wasn't ideal, those extra few hours in close quarters with them was precious. From the middle seat, I lapped up all the physical contact I could get, knowing I wouldn't be able to feel them or breathe them in for a while.

Once we landed, we would walk through the arrivals gate, one child on each side, hands clasped tightly. Until they saw their dad. That's when they'd let go and run to him. He would twirl Cassie and she would squeal. He would give Aidan hugs, reminding him how much he'd missed his big boy. Jason's mother was always in the wings.

From these encounters, I learned that there is strength in numbers. It was difficult to be alone at these hand-offs. I would feel my past anxieties creeping back in. I'd stand, holding their bags, waiting my turn for their attention to say my proper goodbyes.

'Guys, can I get a big hug before you leave with Daddy?' I'd ask. They'd walk over and wrap their little arms around me, letting go all too quickly.

'That's it? Cassie-Bear? Come on, I want a real hug.'

'Urghhhhhh.'

'Go give your mother a hug, Cassie,' Jason would say, crossing his arms over his chest.

I'd kneel, and she would grudgingly turn back and wrap her arms around my neck. I'd squeeze tightly, telling her I loved her. She'd then pull away and jump into his arms again.

'Aidan, come on, bubs, Mommy wants a hug. Make it a good one.'

I'd pull him in close, kiss his head and whisper, 'I love you, kiddo.'

Letting go, he'd mumble quietly, 'Love you too.'

'Come on, guys, let's go. Granny and Grandad invited the family over for dinner so we can celebrate your return. Granny even made a cake. Oh! and I have a surprise for you both at home,' Jason would say, distracting them.

Watching them walk away, I'd silently pray that they would turn around and wave, but they never did. It was as if I no longer existed. I vanished as soon as they were back home. 'Home,' they were continually reminded, could only be the house in which they were born. 'Home' was with their dad.

The flights back to Calgary were my solace, affording me a safe place to let the tears fall after the cabin lights were dimmed. I'd cry for them, knowing that they no longer had a full-time mommy. I cried for myself, for the loss of my place in their lives, for the role I'd taken on as an outsider looking in. How long would it be before they forgot I would always be their mother? How long until I was replaced by their grandmother as the maternal figure in their lives?

Airport drop-offs never got easier. One flight blended into another. I travelled as often as I could to have stolen moments with them. A quick four-day weekend was never enough. These small pockets of time barely allowed us to get through the 'Mommy broke our family' conversations. No sooner had we taken one precious step beyond these interactions and slipped into a softer place where I was just their mother and they were just my kids, and our time would be up. And I would have to leave. Again. It was the only constant in their lives: Mommy leaving.

Summer months, in which we could stay longer in this gentler place, were the only meaningful times we had together. But even these peaceful moments were contaminated by divorce poison with every phone or Skype call. Each one was a small scratch, slowly peeling away at the hard-won tenderness we had created. They were never allowed to forget that once they turned twelve, they had a say as to whether or not they wanted to spend time with me. While this is not the law, the Canadian courts take into consideration a child's preference once they are over the age of twelve.

I began to dread this milestone and fear that the damage of the past would finally catch up with me.

The Park

During the months following the first summer with my kids, I would sometimes take the long way home from work so I could walk past the park. I'd sit on the bench and watch other people's kids running around and playing. I'd close my eyes, remembering what it was like when mine were here. It would always seem like a lifetime ago, even though it was always just a few weeks back.

I replayed Aidan making his way across the monkey bars, his grip slipping part way through. He'd landed on his feet, rubbed his hands together and told me in great detail why he couldn't make it all the way across even though he was strong enough—he was just *too heavy*. I'd moved him just before Cassie had a chance to kick him in the head as she plowed her way through, making it to the other platform.

She'd jumped down, a mischievous glint in her eyes, and announced she was stronger than him because she could do it. He'd insisted she just got lucky and couldn't do it again. She'd wiped her hands on her skirt, saying, 'It's better if your hands are dry,' and glided once again from bar to bar like a little monkey.

She'd landed with a thud, turned around and bowed. I could always tell when Aidan was getting upset.

'Let's go home and make lunch.' Fajitas, his favorite. He'd wrapped his arms around my hips and hugged me tight. We walked home, three-wide, holding hands.

I replayed the memories of the summer spent together in my head, like a movie reel.

I opened my eyes to the bright sun, tears threatening to fall, and had to coax myself to get home to make dinner. Back at the apartment, I threw my bag on the floor, took off my shoes and looked through the mail. Nothing. I had hoped for a letter or a drawing by now. I had given them a stack of stamped envelopes with our address so they could just stuff in a letter or drawing and drop it in the mailbox.

Dustin got home from work as I was chopping vegetables in the kitchen. He greeted me with a kiss on the cheek. 'How was your day?' he asked.

I hesitated. 'I walked by the park on my way home.'

'Oh, honey, I don't know why you do that, it only makes it worse.'

I looked down, blinking the tears away, and mumbled, 'I know.'

'I'm gonna go change and then I'll make you a martini, okay?'

'Sounds good,' I responded, a forced smile on my lips.

I heard his footsteps stop as he walked past Aidan's bedroom. He'd see that the bedding was crumpled up and I still hadn't washed the kids' clothes they'd left here.

Dammit, I thought, *I really should have cleaned that up before he got home.*

He came back into the kitchen, wrapped his arms around me from behind and nuzzled into my neck. 'I love you,' he whispered.

I turned to kiss him. 'I love you, too.'

Dustin never judged my grief. It didn't ease the pain of being without my children, but it allowed me to feel it completely.

The more I was able to lean into every emotion as it came up, the more our relationship deepened and I felt safe enough to be my authentic self.

All The Things That Are Lost

I stirred Aidan awake as the plane began its descent and turned off Cassie's iPod. Another summer had come and gone. We huddled closely, knowing that it would be a few months before we saw each other again. 'I'm really gonna miss you guys,' I whispered, kissing the tops of their heads. They were now eight and ten.

'We don't have to say bye now, Mommy. We're still in the plane,' Cassie said, pulling herself away.

'I know, lovebug, but I like to say bye now and get my hugs and kisses in. Once we get off the plane, there'll be lots of people excited to see you.'

'Mommy, do you have to go back?' Aidan, asked, his eyes insistent under the brim of his hat.

'I do, kiddo. I have to go to work on Monday.' He sighed, turning away. I squeezed him in tighter. 'I'm sorry, A. But I will be back to visit you for Thanksgiving. That's only nine weeks away.'

He stared across the aisle, ignoring me. I took his hand and squeezed it three times. *I. Love. You.* I waited. He didn't squeeze back, but he didn't pull away.

At arrivals, Jason and his mother were waiting at the bottom of the stairs. Cassie pulled her hand out of mine and ran towards him. Jason's mom smiled at Aidan, avoiding my gaze. He let go of my hand and walked to them slowly, his head hung.

'Where's my hug, kiddo?' Jason asked him. 'Is that a new hat?' he continued, tugging at the brim of his ballcap.

'Yeah, DJ bought it for me when we went to the football game.'

'Oh yeah? And what about the hat I sent you with? Did you leave it there?' Aidan looked at me, biting his lower lip. He seemed nervous.

'It's in here,' I said, handing over the plastic bag Jason had sent with them over a month ago. He always sent a single plastic bag to carry the few belongings they were allowed to bring. I had wanted to buy them each a proper backpack, but I feared it would get lost or tossed out, as seemed to be the case with everything we gave them that went back to their father's house.

Jason patted Aidan's head. 'So, is this your favorite hat now?'

Aidan's shoulders dropped and I felt my face get hot. 'No, I still like my other one more,' he said, looking at me shyly.

'You're allowed to have more than one favorite, you know.' I paused. 'Alright, guys, come give me big hugs.'

Cassie held Jason's hand, ignoring me. Aidan slowly stepped forward. I kissed the top of his head and squeezed him tight. He squeezed back before slowly pulling away. I tugged at the brim of his hat and smiled. 'I'll see you in nine weeks, okay? And we'll Skype on Sunday.'

He nodded. I crouched to his level and took his hands in mine. 'I'm gonna miss you, bubs, but I'll see you very soon.' I squeezed his hands three times. Slight smile and he squeezed back four times. *I. Love. You. Too.*

'Cassie-bear, come give me a hug and a kiss,' I said, walking towards her. She hid behind Jason, who had his arms folded over his chest. I tried to catch her arm, but she ran behind her grandmother, giggling. I could feel the people standing around watching us. 'Cassie, come on, sweetheart. Just one kiss and one hug. Please?' Desperation crept into my voice.

Jason unfolded his arms and motioned to Cassie. 'Okay, Princess, enough playing. Go give your mother a hug and a kiss. You won't see her for a long time,' he said, loudly.

I bit the inside of my cheek. It seemed unnecessarily hurtful to keep reminding them of what they were losing every time we exchanged goodbyes. She walked slowly to me, dragging her feet. I picked her up, kissed her cheek and whispered, 'Love you, boo-bear.'

'Love you too,' she said, wriggling out of my arms. Running back to Jason, she asked, 'Daddy, what's that surprise you said you have for me?'

'I'll tell you when we get to the car.' He turned to his mom, holding Aidan's hand, and said, 'Let's go.'

I smiled at Aidan, but he wasn't looking at me. I called out 'Bye, guys!' and waved, but neither turned around. My heart was heavy as I walked back to the departures gate. All these instances of watching them walk away were taking their toll on me. I held the memories of our time together delicately, afraid that if I closed my fists around them too tightly they'd eventually break. My thread of intimacy with them was so tenuous and threatened all the time that I feared pushing for one more hug, kiss or wave goodbye might be our undoing.

•••

'Aidaaaaannnn, it's your turn to talk to Mommy,' Cassie called out towards the hallway. 'Bye Mommy, love you,' she said, standing up.

'Love you too, sweet girl.' I blew kisses at the screen, and she ran off laughing.

I heard his footsteps in the hallway. The laptop was set up on the coffee table, and I could hear Jason making dinner in the kitchen. Aidan's pants appeared as he stood in front of the laptop. The TV was on in the background. He sat, his focus elsewhere.

'Hey, kiddo, can you turn the TV down a bit?' I asked. He rolled his eyes but turned it down slightly.

'Mommy, I don't want to talk long.'

I looked at Dustin over my laptop. He mouthed 'sorry,' and I sighed.

'That's okay, A, I wasn't going to keep you long. I just wanted to say hi and see how the new school year is going. Do you like your new teacher?'

'Mm-hmm. She's nice.' His focus remained on the TV playing behind the laptop screen.

I tried again. 'Did you tell your friends about the football game that we went to? About the fans wearing watermelons as helmets on their heads?'

'No, I didn't.'

'Oh, well, maybe you can tell them about it when you wear your new hat to school.'

He shifted uncomfortably. 'About that,' he started, looking towards the kitchen, where I could hear his dad was moving around. 'Ummm, I lost it.'

I frowned. 'What do you mean, you lost it?'

He sat on his hands, shifting his weight from side to side. 'Well, ummm, it's like this. I thought that I hung it on the hook at the front door, but it wasn't there the next morning.'

'Okay, so it must be somewhere in the house, or maybe in the car. Did you ask Daddy if he put it away somewhere? Maybe Granny moved it when she came over to clean?'

'Yeah. Daddy says I probably lost it on my way home from the airport.'

'That makes no sense, Aidan, you had it on your head. I'm sure it's somewhere in the house if—'

'Dinner is ready, guys,' I heard Jason calling out. 'Aidan, say bye to your mother, it's time to eat.'

'I have to hang up now, Daddy said it's time to eat.'

'Okay, but promise me that—' I didn't get to finish my sentence before the call was dropped.

'Un-fucking-believable.' I got up so quickly that the chair hit the wall behind me.

'Are you really surprised?' Dustin asked. 'Anything we give them ends up "lost" or "stolen."'

'He loved that freaking hat. He wore it from morning to night all summer. I had to force him to take it off in restaurants.' I slumped on the sofa, resting my head on Dustin's shoulder. 'I don't get it. It's not just me he's punishing, it's the kids, too.'

'They're getting older, babe. They'll start figuring it out soon.'

Eat, Drink and Be Married

Dustin and I had been living together for six months when he proposed. We were on a vacation in Mexico, celebrating his birthday. We sat on the beach in the early evening light, looking out at the sun starting its slow descent behind the ocean. Taking the last sip of his beer, he turned to me.

'Sonia, I love you. I have always loved you and I always will.' I smiled and leaned over to kiss him. I started to speak, but he put his hand up to shush me. He dug in the sand between his legs and pulled out a ring. 'Will you marry me?'

I squealed. 'Yes. Oh my god. Yes.' We kissed and he put the ring on my finger. A perfect fit. The rest of the trip passed in a warm haze. We were as giddy as children, drunk on love and Dos Equis.

He suggested recreating the proposal when the kids were with us for spring break. The night we picked them up from the airport, he took them aside.

'I'm going to ask your mommy to marry me, and I need your help.' They were excited.

He got up early with them the next morning, insisting that I stay in bed. I could hear the giggles in the kitchen as they made breakfast.

The three of them barged into the bedroom and clambered onto the bed. I pretended to be half-asleep and surprised about my breakfast in bed.

'Wow, who made all of this?'

'We did. Well, DJ cooked the stuff, but I helped him put it on the tray,' Aidan said, with a big, toothy grin.

'Mommy, put some sugar in your coffee,' Cassie insisted, pushing the sugar bowl towards me. 'Open it, Mommy, here.'

Aidan shoved her. 'Stop it. Don't ruin the surprise,' he whispered.

Dustin smiled as I reached for the sugar bowl. I opened it and Cassie squealed. 'Look, there's a ring.' She took it out and handed it to me. Aidan rolled his eyes and punched her arm.

'What is this?' I feigned shock.

'DJ wants to marry you,' Cassie blurted out.

Dustin smiled. 'Well, will you marry me?'

I said yes all over again. We kissed and he put the ring on my finger.

We didn't want a big wedding, just something low-key, with all the kids present, his and mine, as well as my parents and some of his siblings. His 'best man' was his best girlfriend, Diana. I asked my stepdaughter, Ally, to be my maid of honor.

We were married on December 29, 2012, at the Blue Star Diner, our favorite restaurant. It was a crisp winter evening. Fresh snow covered the ground. We all walked together from our house down to the restaurant. Dustin carried Cassie on his back, and I held Aidan's hand. Cassie had my vows in her purse to help me in case I forgot them. Aidan held the rings. Ally stood by my side, and Diana stood by his. We recited our vows in front of our kids, my parents, his sister and a handful of friends. It was perfect. After the short ceremony, we ate sliders, chicken wings and curly fries. We drank wine and beer and celebrated our love. I remember every single minute of it.

Later, we all walked back to our house and shared desserts. I rubbed Aidan's back as he threw up from over-indulging on spicy chicken wings and chocolate cake, and Cassie stayed up dancing in the living room with the adults until the wee hours of the morning. And just like that, DJ earned his title. Stepdad.

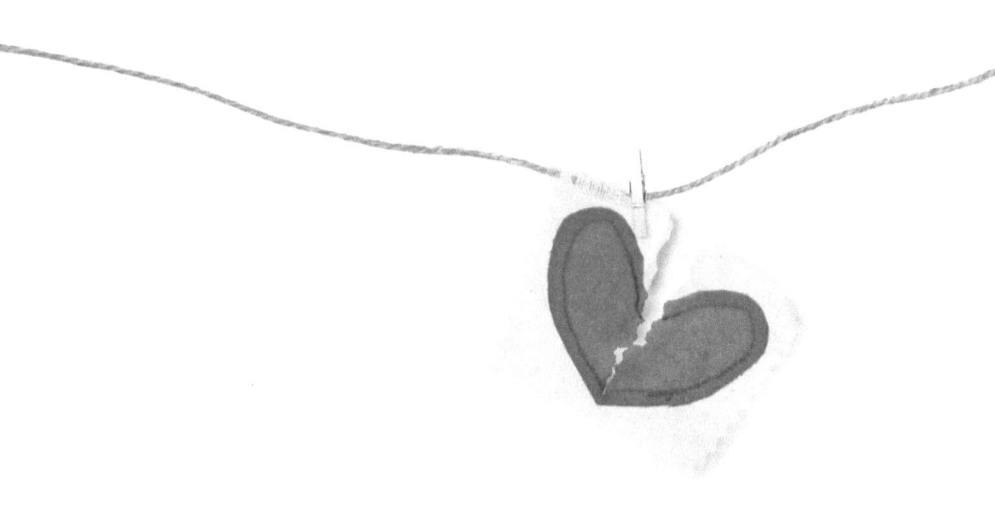

Skype

I was on my usual Sunday Skype call with the kids. Cassie was showing me some of the stuffed animals she was playing with. Her attention kept shifting from the computer screen to the TV show playing in the background.

'Can you turn the TV down a bit, baby-girl? I'm having a hard time hearing you.'

She looked over to the left and said that she couldn't because Daddy and Aidan were watching the show.

I asked if she could take the laptop to her bedroom. 'That way we can talk to each other without so many disruptions. And you can show me more of your stuffies and tell me their names.' Her eyes darted to the left again.

'No, I can't, Mommy. Daddy says the computer is going to die if I unplug it.'

I stretched my neck. 'Okay, well, can you put on the special headphones that Mommy bought you guys for Skyping?'

She played with her hands in her lap. 'It's 'cause, I don't know where they are.'

I looked at Dustin over the screen of the laptop. I could feel my jaw clenching, my face hot.

'It's okay, sweet girl.' I smiled. 'What do you want to talk about now?' I asked, trying to sound cheerful.

'Well, ummm. Mommy, I really want to watch this show. Can I say bye now?'

I sighed. 'Okay, lovebug. Can you please put Aidan on so I can talk to him for a bit?'

She looked to the left, nodding. 'Ummm, it's 'cause ... ummm, Aidan will Skype you after the show is done.' She nodded again. 'In about twenty minutes.'

It was frustrating. 'Okay. Can you ask Daddy to text me when Aidan's ready so I can turn Skype back on?'

'K, bye.'

'Love you, Cas—' The call dropped.

I looked at Dustin. 'Something weird is going on, babe. I can feel it in my bones.'

I sent Jason a text message. *Can you please make sure that Aidan does Skype me tonight? I haven't been able to connect with him the last few times.*

I sat and stared at the computer screen, waiting. Aidan had become more and more distant lately. He never wanted to talk on the phone when I called. He was almost twelve, and I understood that, at that age, the last thing he wanted was to chat with his mom, but it still hurt. And the last few Skype calls he'd either not been home or had been too busy to talk. I'd been lucky to get a 'Hi! Bye!' from him.

Half an hour passed and I texted Jason again. *Is he almost ready?*

My phone pinged. *Now.* The call connected and the screen turned on. I smiled.

'Hey, kiddo. How are you?'

He stared back at me stone-faced. I tilted my head to the side, still smiling. 'Hi,' I tried again.

'I don't want to come out at Christmas time. I want to stay home.' I glanced at Dustin, who stood up and turned the football game down.

'What do you mean, A? Why don't you want to come?' I searched his face on the screen.

'Because. I don't want to, and you can't make me. I'm old enough to decide if I want to or not.' He looked at me sternly through the screen.

My fists tightened in my lap. I took a breath, trying to stay calm. 'You can't just make that decision without having a conversation with me, kiddo.'

'Yeah, I can. Daddy says that when I'm twelve years old I can decide if I see you or not, and I don't want to go to Calgary at Christmas time.' His eyes were defiant. Twelve, the magic number, was almost upon us.

My chest felt like it was on fire. The room was spinning. I couldn't swallow. Dustin walked closer to hear what Aidan was saying. The walls started closing in. 'Actually, Aidan, that's not true. And even if it was, you're not going to be twelve years old until next spring,' I said, my voice angrier than I meant it to be.

'I don't want to come, and you can't make me,' he responded, still stone-faced. I noticed him looking up over the computer screen.

I took a sharp breath and rolled my shoulders. 'Can we talk about something else for now and decide later about Christmas?'

His gaze moved up over the screen again. 'There's nothing to decide. I'm not coming, and you can't make me.'

I snapped. 'You know what, Aidan, that's not true. I can make you. I can call my lawyers and I can have them file a motion before a judge that will force you to come out and see us at the agreed-upon times. And if you don't fly when you're supposed to, you will be in contempt of court. Do you know what that means, kiddo? You seem to know so much about your legal rights, I'm sure that someone has told you what being in contempt of court means.'

His face softened, his eyes watering.

All of a sudden Jason's face appeared on the screen. 'Sonia, I will not have you threaten my son. Do you understand me.' He sat next to Aidan, wrapping his arm around his shoulders and pulling him in for a hug. *I fucking knew it. This was a trap.* I shook with anger.

'Have you been standing there, listening in on this entire conversation?' I threw my hands up. 'Why am I surprised? You're always lurking in the background, listening in. I haven't had a private conversation with the kids since I moved out here.'

He looked offended. 'I don't listen in on your conversations,' he scoffed. 'But when I hear you threatening my son, I—'

'OUR son, Jason,' I shouted. 'Pretty sure he's mine too! Pretty sure I remember birthing him!'

'When I hear you threatening our son, I will step in to defend him.'

Aidan pulled away, looking uncomfortable. I heard Cassie calling out in the background. 'Go back to bed, Princess. Daddy will be there in a minute.'

'I wasn't threatening him, Jason. Look, I'm not doing this. Not tonight.'

I turned to look directly at Aidan. 'Listen, A, we can talk about this another day, okay? Right now, we are not in the right mood to have a good conversation. So let's just say goodnight and we can talk about it later.'

He looked down at his hands. 'Okay. Bye, Mommy.'

'Goodnight kiddo. I lo—' the call got dropped.

My whole body was shaking. I looked at Dustin, tears pooling in the corners of my eyes. 'He fucking planned this. This whole thing tonight, it was a setup. I can't believe I fell for it.'

'It's okay, babe. You handled it well.'

'No I didn't. I completely lost my shit. That was not cool.' I put my face in my hands and rubbed my cheeks. 'Why couldn't Jason just tell me that Aidan was thinking about not coming? Why can't he ever just talk to me about these things, instead of letting the kids spring them up on me like that?' I shook my head, hot tears rolling down my face.

'Hon, what are you doing?' Dustin asked as I picked up my phone.

I wiped my cheeks. 'I'm texting Jason. I'm going to be an adult and try to co-parent like normal, civilized, divorced people who care more about their kids than their hatred for each other would do.'

I typed, *Look, I messed up tonight. I shouldn't have reacted that way. Can you and I please have a conversation, by phone and not text, to talk about this? I know that Aidan thinks he has final say on the matter, but I think it's best for you and me to discuss these topics before they get dropped in my lap.* I hit send and put the phone down.

A few hours later, my phone dinged. **1 new message:** *Ok*.

Although we had a custody agreement which specifically outlined my access to the kids in terms of calls, Skypes and in-person visits, I spent years at Jason's mercy when it came to this access. He had the power to decide if and when I could speak to them. Angry words on my part were met with unanswered calls on his. Skype calls were cut short, and care packages I sent sat in the mailbox for days even after I'd notify them they had been delivered. I bowed down and continually gave in to him, for fear that the little bit of access he allowed me would be taken away. I contacted my lawyer and was told that there wasn't much we could do, other than bring the matter in front of a judge. As long as he could prove that he was doing everything in his power to ensure I had my rightful access, we would gain nothing. So, each time I was told that the kids were busy, or sleeping, or didn't feel like talking or Skyping, I'd remind myself that this power he held over me was temporary.

The kids would eventually be old enough to communicate with me directly. I just hoped that day would come before irretrievable damage was done to my relationship with them.

Photographs

That Christmas, Aidan ended up settling on visiting for five days, while Cassie stayed for twelve. During the following scheduled visit—spring break—she came alone; Aidan went to hockey camp instead.

Cassie, now almost ten, had asked if she could make a photo album to bring back to her dad's. 'For when I miss you,' she had said when I was tucking her in on one of the last nights before she left.

It was early and she was still sleeping, so I brought my coffee mug upstairs and pulled out the boxes of photographs I had on the top shelf of the walk-in closet. It had been ages since I'd looked in them. I sat on the bedroom floor and opened the first box.

I found pictures of Aidan at two months. Jason is feeding him but has his hands up to show that Aidan is strong enough to hold the bottle on his own.

Another of Aidan tucked into the corner of the sofa, a big smile on his face. I remembered putting this one in a frame for my parents because they had bought him that little outfit. I looked through them quickly, and almost all were of Aidan at various stages of his childhood.

Then there was one of me and Jason on the sofa at his parents' house, Aidan sitting between us. Our faces are soft. Fulfilled. I have a half smile, looking at Aidan, while Jason gazes into the camera. I couldn't remember who took this picture, but we looked happy. I put it back in and closed the lid.

In the next box I found one of me in my grey maternity shirt. Aidan is standing in front of me, lifting my shirt, kissing my pregnant belly. 'Kiss the baby, Mommy.' It didn't matter where we were; when he wanted to kiss the baby, my shirt went up and he kissed my tummy. He liked pressing his face up against my belly when she kicked. It made him laugh so hard. In that photo I can see my face is tired.

I found a dozen pictures from Cassie's baby shower. I was much smaller with her than when I was pregnant with Aidan. I knew she was a girl before the ultrasound confirmed it. The two pregnancies were so different.

There were a few of Cassie as a newborn at the hospital, peacefully bundled up in my mom's arms. One of me, sitting in the hospital bed, wearing glasses, my hair messy. I examined the picture more closely. I am smiling but it does not reach my eyes. There were more pictures of baby Cassie. Some with Jason, Aidan, and all of us. Seeing these images, I realized that the first two months of her life were a blur for me. I don't remember any of these moments captured in photographs. No one warned me that two children would be so much harder than one. In the midst of those dark times I had felt so lost, I didn't think I'd ever find a way out. In time, I would come to learn that even the hardest moments are only temporary and I am strong enough to get through them.

I opened the last box. More of the same. Birthdays, Easters, Christmas, all of the holidays. In the photos, we are smiling, but something about them is different. These were the pictures Jason left on my doorstep after I moved out—photos of our past, with letters written to me on the back of them speaking of heartbreak, betrayal, a man broken, a family ruined. He'd also left me the candles from our wedding day that signified our union. They were broken, like our vows. One night, I had come home to find our entire wedding album on my doorstep. I had considered burning it but stowed it away in case the kids ever wanted to look through it.

Cassie and I spent the afternoon putting the album together. She asked me questions about the photos she chose. I told her stories about when she was younger, but it was harder to find stories for the last few years, since I'd moved away.

'Is it okay for me to take some of the wedding photos? Of you and Daddy. You look so pretty in your dress. Like a princess,' she asked.

'Of course. That's why I kept them.'

Every night before bed she looked through the album. 'I'm going to ask Daddy if I can put pictures of him and the family too. That way, I'll never miss anyone.'

'What a great idea,' I told her.

It made me wonder if the concept of family was less contentious for Cassie because she was only two when her dad and I separated. Although she and Aidan were fed the same the narrative about 'family,' she had no real recollection of us all living under one roof. Over the years, she often questioned whether the stories and moments she remembered were her own or if they had been communicated to her by others.

A few weeks later, over the phone, she told me she could no longer find her photo album. It wasn't in the hiding spot she had put it, not in her closet, or under the bed. She'd asked her dad and her granny if they'd seen it. They hadn't; she must've misplaced it.

The following winter she texted me to say that she had found it. It was tucked in under all the winter accessories on the very top shelf of the hallway closet. She would never have found it if she hadn't taken everything down while searching for a specific wool headband she wanted to wear for her ski day.

New message from Cassie: *I hid it in my bedroom. Hopefully it doesn't get *lost* again.*

I responded with a sad-face emoji. I felt her frustration and disappointment from three thousand kilometers away. Putting the phone down on the counter, I rested my head in my hands and smiled. Dustin was right. In the end, the kids would make up their own minds. They'd work out their own truths.

While my relationship with Cassie was strengthening, Aidan continued pulling away from me. It started slowly, with him spending shorter times in Calgary. He didn't want to chat when I phoned, and the quality of our Skype calls deteriorated. As his visits grew shorter, Cassie's grew longer. One summer, we planned a month-long trip to Hawaii. Aidan opted not to come—he had been promised hockey camps. Cassie was all-in. Dustin, Cassie and I spent a peaceful month lying by the pool and watching the sunsets. We ate, swam, explored and practiced yoga daily. Being with her was effortless; I didn't have to try hard.

When Aidan was around, I'd feel my defenses springing up, as if I constantly had to justify my decision to move away. I was forever trying to earn his love and affection. I wanted so badly for our relationship to be like it had been before the separation. I longed for the closeness we had shared for the first four years of his life. But it's a virtually impossible task to earn your child's affection. I thought that a mother could rely on the love of her children—that it was guaranteed. I had carried him as a baby in my womb, and I believed that bond couldn't be broken. It was a tough lesson to learn how fragile the relationship between mother and child can be.

Zurich

Dustin was offered a role in the Swiss office at a time when the oil and gas industry was crashing—and we desperately needed the job. Zurich was only an extra two hours by airplane than Calgary—six instead of four. I kept telling myself that it was do-able. The kids had become accustomed to flying to see us. Dustin accepted the offer. We put the house on the market and started dreaming of a retirement in a European city. It sounded magical. We decided to tell the kids over the Christmas break. What I did not consider was how the six-hour time difference might affect our communications.

Cassie was enthusiastic at the thought of traveling around Europe. She insisted we take all her belongings with us—her toys, bed, everything. Aidan didn't react, other than to say it didn't make any difference to him where we lived.

'But you'll come and visit?' I asked.

'Depends on my hockey schedule and stuff.'

Moving from Calgary to Zurich meant we had to downsize considerably.

We were going from a five-bedroom house to a two-bedroom apartment. We hosted a wine and cheese event for our friends and colleagues on a Sunday afternoon, a quick-fire gathering where we put out what we had to sell or give away. Everything was gone—even some of the items I had meant to keep.

I noticed Dustin, Diana and her young son, Connor, heading down to the basement. I had laid out some of the toys and kids' books Cassie had given me the green light to give away.

Aidan didn't want us to move any of his things to Zurich. 'It's not really my stuff anyway. I never use it,' he had said.

'What do you mean, it's not your stuff? We moved it from Glengarry to Calgary, kiddo, and you used to play with this all the time. You're even wearing it in the photos Ally took of us,' I had said, pulling out his Bakugan arm band.

He'd chuckled. 'Yeah, but that was a long time ago, and I don't need that stuff anymore. Besides, I haven't been here much and I'm probably not going to come to Zurich.'

I'd sighed. 'You sure?'

'Yeah, I'm sure.'

I'd put out his belongings on the basement table that morning, blinking back the tears. I'd picked up the two stuffed dogs that he used to sleep with and breathed them in. I couldn't bring myself to throw them out or give them away, so I'd put them in Cassie's toy chest. *Maybe he'll change his mind someday and want these,* I told myself.

Dustin and Diana came back up the stairs as I was loading the dishwasher. I wiped my hands and turned around. Diana had a few kids' books and toys in her hands, and Connor was dragging the purple beanbag chair behind him.

I looked at Dustin. 'Hey, where's Cassie's beanbag chair going?'

'Oh, Connor wanted it, so I told him he could take it.'

I wiped my mouth with the back of my hand. 'But ... Cassie wanted to keep it.'

'Babe, where are we going to put it? It's a small apartment, and there's no room in the second bedroom for it.'

'Well, what if we stored it under the bed in the guest room or in the storage locker? Cassie was clear that she wanted us to move all her stuff.'

'We can get another one in Zurich if she really misses it that much,' Dustin said, following Connor out the front door. I watched as he loaded the beanbag chair in the trunk of Diana's car and closed it. He hugged her tightly and waved as they drove away.

'Well, that was a success,' he said, closing the front door. We had managed to get rid of all the items we weren't taking with us. The few odds and ends that were left would be taken to the donation center after the movers packed everything up.

'Mmm-hmmm. It was.'

He wrapped his arms around me from behind and I pulled away. 'You okay?'

I picked up some plates from the counter. 'Why did you give Connor the beanbag chair?'

'I told you, he wanted it. And I didn't think that we were moving it to Zurich.'

'You should have asked me before giving it away.'

'Babe, why are you so upset about this? It's just a beanbag chair.'

I turned to face him. 'It's not JUST a beanbag chair. It's *Cassie's* beanbag chair.' I looked down, blinking back the tears.

'You're right. I'm sorry. I should have asked you first. I just, I didn't think that we were bringing it with us.' He pulled me close and I sank into his chest.

When I moved to Calgary in 2010, I'd packed up my entire apartment and shipped it, including all the kids' furniture, clothes and toys. Whenever I missed them, I would look through their toys, smell their clothes and lie in their beds. This made me feel somehow closer to them. Every time I donated the clothes they had outgrown, I felt like I was losing a small piece of them. I wanted every single card, drawing and piece of art or craft that the kids had given me to come with us. I placed bits of papers with scribbles and doodles and *xoxo* notes in a special box and cherished them, as though they were precious gems. I would look at these treasures often to remind myself that I was a good and devoted mother and that my kids did love me, even though I wasn't physically present every day. These were my lifelines, and having to give them up was like suffering the loss of my connection to my children, over and over each time.

I knew we would not have room for the beanbag chair and that Cassie probably wouldn't be upset that we had given it away. It wasn't about the beanbag chair. It was about me losing yet another memento that reminded me of my children.

•••

We arrived in Zurich on March 4, 2016, with nine suitcases, two carry-ons and two small dogs in carrier bags. We were both exhausted and elated. We could not believe how fortunate we were to be able to live in Switzerland.

While the outside of our apartment had an old-world feel, the inside had been completely remodelled into a bright, modern, open-concept space with two bedrooms, a large living room, office, dining room and kitchen, complete with an American-sized refrigerator. The best features of the apartment were the wood-burning fireplace and the expansive, partly covered terrace overlooking Lake Zurich. Even though it was snowing, we stood on the terrace, popped open the bottle of champagne our landlord had left us and toasted to our new beginning.

But adjusting to life there was harder than I had expected. It's one experience to visit a city for one week and see it as a tourist. It's entirely another to move to a new environment and work out how to fit in. Our shipment took three months to arrive from Canada, but once we were unpacked, it started to feel more or less like home. I'd walk around the apartment, pick up mementos and look at photos, feeling incredibly homesick. I'd scroll through the social media feeds of my friends and family and wonder if they missed me as much as I missed them. I had not realized how much of my self-worth I attached to my job and relationships. Dustin was busy adjusting to his new role in the Swiss office and so I hid my sadness, not wanting to burden him with it.

Luckily, summer came quickly, and Cassie arrived for her first visit. She brought so much life to the apartment during those two months. We spent most of our days down by the lake and wandering around town. We ate shawarmas on the cobblestone steps facing Lake Zurich. We walked up and down narrow streets, chasing Pokémons. I was sad that Aidan hadn't come, but I rejoiced in Cassie's company. I didn't feel guilty about giving her all my attention, and she delighted in it.

We took her to Paris, Normandy and London. We visited all the sights and ate all the food. We stayed up late and got up early, soaking in as much of the culture as we could. We went on an impromptu girls-only side trip to Milan. We shopped, did some sightseeing, and ate pizza.

One night before her return, Cassie looked up at me with hesitation. 'I was wondering, do you think I could come and live here? With you and DJ?'

My breath caught. I felt a slow smile tugging at my lips. I turned to Dustin, who nodded. I walked over and took a seat next to her, wrapping my arms around her small frame. She leaned into me and I kissed her forehead.

'Of course, lovebug. We would love to have you with us,' I said, unable to tone down my excitement. 'You'll have to talk to Daddy, though. He'll have to be okay with that.'

She nodded quietly. 'I know.' The mood became somber.

We sat in silence for a few minutes before Dustin spoke up. 'A lot of the expat kids who come here go to international schools. A few of the people who are in my office were saying that they're pretty cool.'

Her face lit up. 'Could I still learn German at an international school?'

'I'm sure you could.'

That night in bed, I allowed myself to imagine what it might be like to have her with me all the time. I pictured myself making her breakfast, packing her lunches, and taking her back-to-school shopping. I'd meet her at the train station, and we could get lattes and walk home together. I could help her with homework and teach her how to make some of her favorite meals. All the moments I'd missed out on for years were so close, I could almost touch them.

A few weeks after had she returned to Canada, while my excitement was brewing, we Skyped.

'I've changed my mind. I think it's better if I wait. I should probably finish my school here.' Her voice was quiet, and she fiddled with her shirt sleeve. 'It's just that it's not really worth it for a year.'

I nodded, urging her to go on.

'And, well, all my friends are here. And the family is here, too. So, yeah.'

I bit my upper lip. 'Of course, Cassie-bear. I understand.' I blinked back my tears, not wanting to make her feel bad for her change of heart. 'It would be a big change, huge really. Maybe you'll decide to study abroad for college or university.' I forced a smile and asked about her upcoming volleyball tournament.

Meanwhile, I had gotten my hopes up. I'd even started looking into schools. I'd allowed myself to dream of a life with my daughter by my side. After our call ended, I sat alone, reeling from the disappointment that it wasn't going to happen.

I had become used to the silence around me, day in and day out. Dustin would get home, tired from work, hoping to relax, and all I wanted was to talk and hear about his day. I needed to talk. I felt so isolated during that time. I had no friends, no family, and the differing time zones made it hard to connect with any of my loved ones. The loneliness was overwhelming. I longed to fit in and find a community of like-minded people I could connect with. I would see people out and about around town, laughing and talking animatedly, and was envious. I'd sit on the trams and trains listening to people, desperately wishing I could speak Swiss-German so I could join in on the conversations. Once again, I was an outsider looking in.

Dustin and I often went out for lunch or dinner on weekends, but mostly I spent my weekdays in the apartment. I rarely left unless it was to pick up groceries or other essentials. I couldn't get a work visa and struggled with the fact that I was not earning my own money.

•••

The first year in Zurich began to feel like the year after Cassie was born. A fog seeped in and, hard as I tried, I couldn't outrun it. I started to withdraw into myself again. I pulled away from Dustin, not wanting to burden him with my grief and loneliness. I began to have thoughts of running away and trying to find my way back to a life I loved. I missed my friends. I missed my family. I missed my kids. I wondered if we'd made a mistake by moving so far away. Eventually, even the beauty of where we were living was lost on me. All I could focus on was what I was missing. Surrounded by our belongings, I felt a million miles away from home.

I was doing it yet again.

Whenever I'd find myself in a new situation or a place of uncertainty, I'd romanticize the past, longing for a previous 'better' life. I'd forget that even in those former seasons I desperately wished to return to, my life was not as idyllic as I remembered. I'd let the grief of what I'd lost swallow me, and I'd doubt my decisions, convincing myself I'd made a mistake. These intense feelings would paralyze me, plunge me into an all-consuming darkness.

Through therapy, reading and committed self-exploration, I've come to understand that romanticizing the past only robs me of the joy of the present. Life is often hard, and starting anew is never easy. Over time, I've learned how to cherish memories rather than crave a return to the past. I remind myself that I've gotten through hard times before. Life is a series of seasons, some in which the sun feels warm on your skin and others where it rains for weeks on end. Now I work hard to make as many beautiful memories as I can during the happier seasons, so that I can go inward and revisit them during the painful ones.

Dustin saw the toll my isolation was taking. So, after Cassie returned to her dad's, he insisted, despite the expense, that I join a Pilates studio I'd seen advertised on the tram that had English-speaking classes, so I could interact with new people. These classes made a huge difference to my well-being and state of mind.

The first year in Zurich went by quickly. I went to Pilates a few times a week. I flew to Canada as often as I could to see my parents and kids, but the trips always felt too short. I could never have enough time on my own with Aidan and Cassie.

I had what was starting to feel like a routine in my life again. I still struggled with my identity and self-esteem because I wasn't working, but I was slowly understanding that my self-worth could not be attached to a job. I had to find ways to feel good about myself separate from other people. So I started taking writing classes and focused on incorporating daily meditation into my life, and allowing myself to be fully in the season I was in. I began to feel as if I could put roots down in Zurich.

When Aidan agreed to visit the second summer, I was ecstatic. It had been years since we had been together for a substantial amount of time. I hoped we'd reconnect so we could be more active in each other's lives moving forward. Cassie arrived a few weeks before he did. I didn't understand why she wasn't her usual bubbly self. Before her brother arrived, we took a five-day trip to Lisbon, but she seemed irritable and snappy the entire time. I told myself it was probably the teenage hormones finally kicking in. But it wasn't that at all.

Once Aidan arrived, she relaxed. She later confided she had been uncertain how the three of us would coexist. It had been such a long time since we'd all been together in the same house for a long period of time. But as soon as she saw I had more than enough attention for both of them, she became herself again. I'd also been anxious about us sharing the small apartment but set her mind at ease that I'd give them both equally of my time and focus. We spent seventeen days reveling in each other's company. And, like all our reunions, it came to an end with the airport witnessing our hugs goodbye.

I had no idea of the life changes we were all about to undergo or that the hug at the airport would be my last with my son.

I have relived that moment over and over in my head, dissecting and examining each part carefully to see where it broke. I have gone over those seventeen days with a fine-tooth comb, searching for clues I might have missed. I've stared at the photos, asking myself if the smiles are genuine. I've watched the videos of us laughing and cannot believe it was not real. I play the days over and over like a reel, hoping I'll find something to help me understand what happened. I still haven't found it. And even if I did, how can I fix it? How can I change a moment I didn't realize was going to happen?

I wish this story had a happy ending. I long for a warm, bright season with my son, filled with laughter, joy and memory-making, but it hasn't happened.

And so I remind myself: seasons change.

Repeating Betrayals

Daddy knows.

The message lit up on my phone.

I suddenly saw I had several messages and missed FaceTime calls from Cassie. I swiped the screen and read the messages. I sensed the panic in her words.

I didn't tell him but he saw my phone and I hadn't had a chance to delete the messages.

And now he knows and he's super pissed.

He's told everyone and they're all mad at me.

I don't know what to do.

...

Cassie had turned thirteen the summer of 2017 and decided she wanted to come live with us in Zurich. When she'd discussed this possibility with her dad the previous year, she had been met with overwhelming resistance and had changed her mind. But this time she wouldn't be convinced otherwise and had been waiting for the right time to tell Jason.

I re-read the messages, trying to make sense of them. It was close to midnight where she was. She should have been asleep.

Cassie—are you ok? What do you want me to do?

I saw the '...' bubbles and held my breath, waiting for her response.

I don't know what to do. He said I was a liar. He said I was manipulative and conniving. Like you.

My head was spinning. *Liar. Manipulative. Conniving.* Words I had become used to hearing. It wasn't fair to throw them at our daughter. I was overcome with all my own sadness and heartbreak. *Leaving the family. Abandoning us.* All these words from my past came hurtling at me from my daughter's phone. She was committing the ultimate crime. She was choosing to leave. Just as I had.

Cassie, you're not doing anything wrong. Okay? I waited. *Do not let them make you feel bad for this. I'll call the school counsellor again today and make sure she connects with you.*

They're all so sad. And mad. I don't know what to do.

I know honey. I know. Try to get some sleep and text me when you get up. Everything's going to be okay. Now that Dad knows, we can start planning for real.

Dustin walked into the bedroom, surprised to see me sitting up in bed with the light on. 'How come you're up?' My hands were shaking. He sat on the edge of the bed. 'Everything okay?'

'He knows. Jason knows, and he's really pissed.'

'She finally told him? That's a good thing, babe. Now we can really get moving. We knew he wouldn't be happy about this.'

'No, she didn't tell him. He went through her phone and saw some messages. He accused her of being a conniving liar—just like her mother.'

'Oh boy. What do you want to do?'

'I don't know.' A small cry escaped my throat.

He pulled me in to his chest. 'It's alright. We'll figure this out. The circumstances aren't great, but now he knows. And that's probably a good thing.'

I nodded. 'Yes, but I know how he can be when he feels blindsided. I've been there. I don't want her to go through that.'

I spent the day trying to keep busy. I read her messages over and over again. Old anger simmered in my body. How could a father think that it was okay to go through his teenage daughter's phone? Images flashed in my mind of all the times he went through my purse and phone, never respecting my boundaries, asserting his dominance. I remember the experience of violation. I knew just how Cassie was feeling.

Later that day, when Dustin got home, there were still no new messages from her. Had Jason taken her phone away? He'd done it before, confiscated the only link between us because she wouldn't give him the password. I decided to call my parents and tell them what had happened. Maybe she could spend the weekend with them and get away from all the anger and sadness.

My parents were thrilled at the prospect of having a weekend with her and agreed to pick her up after school on Friday. 'She can stay as long as she wants. We can even drive her to school,' my mom said. They knew of her plan to move to Zurich and were ecstatic both for her and for me.

Dustin was sitting at his desk, looking at flights on Expedia. 'Babe, I think you should go to Canada. We can get a decent price for a flight that would get you there Friday night. Around dinner time.'

'I can't leave that quickly. She has to work some of this out with Jason. I emailed him and he hasn't even responded to me.'

'That's why I think you should go. He'll have a harder time ignoring you if you're on his doorstep.'

A few hours later, Cassie and I FaceTimed. She was sitting on her bed, her face pale, deep, dark circles under her eyes. Her hair was in a messy bun. She pulled at the leg of one of her stuffed animals.

'Do you want to tell me what happened last night?' I asked.

She shrugged. 'Dad went through my phone. I had forgotten to delete the messages. And he read them and figured out that I'm moving.' She threw the stuffed animal at her wall. 'I tried to explain it to him, but he wouldn't listen to me. He just said that I had lied and that I had been keeping secrets. I was mad, so I went to my room.'

'I'm sorry, Cassie. Dad shouldn't be going through your phone. Have you talked to him today?'

'Yeah. He sent me a text at lunch to say we will talk more tonight.' She looked toward her bedroom door. 'He's told everyone. I wanted to be the one to tell them, but he told Granny and Grandad and Aidan. And now, they're all mad at me. Granny just keeps crying.'

I clenched my jaw and swallowed hard. I couldn't let him do this to her, I wouldn't let him. 'Listen, honey, I spoke to Mami and Papi, and they said that they would love to spend the weekend with you if you want. I don't want you to have to be around people who are going to go out of their way to make you feel bad about your decision. What do you think?'

'Dad won't like that.'

'Yeah, well, Dad doesn't get to make you feel like an asshole all weekend,' I said, straining to hear if anyone was making a noise in the background. Aidan was probably at home with her.

She sighed. 'Okay, I'll go. Can you tell him, though?'

'Yep, I'll send him a note. Now, talk to Dad tonight, be honest about your feelings and whatever you do, DO NOT let them make you feel bad about this. You're allowed to want to live with me.'

She looked over her shoulder at the hallway. 'Okay. I gotta hang up. I have a lot of homework to do and I'm super tired from not sleeping last night. I'll text you before I go to bed.'

In bed that night, I couldn't stop thinking about Cassie. I'd been in the same position before, making decisions that were right for me without support from my loved ones. I knew how difficult it was to stay true to your convictions in the face of negative responses. It's hard to be around people who are disappointed in you. It's exhausting to try and convince others that your choices matter, that perhaps, you know what's best for you.

Unlike Cassie, I wasn't faced with difficult decisions at a young age—only later in life. She'd watched me make many of them. I know that my choices were hard for her to accept, but maybe witnessing her own mother stand her ground emboldened her to do the same. Perhaps watching me choose the life I knew I deserved gave her the courage to take action. My daughter must have learned from me that, sometimes, the unpopular choice is the one that saves you. The only way to live an authentic life is to do what's right for you, by trusting that small whisper when it tells you you're capable of being big and bold.

I woke the next morning to messages from both Cassie and Jason. They had talked and, while he did not agree with her moving, he conceded that ultimately it was her choice. He would never stop her from seeing her grandparents, so she could stay with them for the weekend. I replied that we should probably talk about dates for the move. He responded that he wasn't ready for that.

'I need a few weeks to digest her decision.'

I read and re-read his email several times, trying to decipher what he was actually saying. We had such a difficult history of continually mistrusting one another that I struggled to believe he would get back to me soon or that he wouldn't take this time to pressure her into changing her mind.

I decided that Dustin was right—I needed to get there; otherwise he might drag his feet. I was on a plane the next day. I'd always told my kids that I was just a flight away, and now I got to prove it. Landing in Ottawa after my long journey across the ocean, I grabbed a coffee and drove the hour from the airport to my parents' house, where Cassie was spending the weekend. I walked up the stairs and into the main living area. She was sitting in the rocking chair, watching a movie.

When she turned and saw me standing by the sofa, she was taken aback. 'What?!?! How?!?! What?!?' She looked to my parents, then back to me. 'But ...' she ran to hug me.

'I thought you might want me to be here to help you talk to your dad,' I said, kissing the top of her head. She pulled away, tears rolling down her cheeks. I hugged her tight and whispered, 'I've always told you that I'm only a flight away.'

• • •

When Cassie made the decision to move to Zurich, she had to endure emotionally tense discussions with Jason and his side of the family. They did not want her to go, and so they couldn't support her at a time when she really needed them to. It seemed a shock to everyone that she and I had maintained such a close bond over time and distance. I had worked hard to cultivate a loving relationship with her by sending care packages, almost daily messages and making sure to always be present when I was with her. I had tried to do the same with Aidan, but because we were spending less and less time together, it had been more difficult. Cassie and I maintained regular contact as she got older, especially once she had her own phone.

I had never tried to persuade her to come and live with me, but I made sure she knew we always had a home for her. I never wanted her to feel like she had to pick between me or her dad again. I had never wanted either of my kids to ever feel that pressure.

But as the years went by, she had become curious about the separation and had begun asking me questions. I could see her grappling to put the pieces her dad had given her together with the ones I was giving her, as she tried to create a more complete picture. I had spent the last seven years wishing I had my kids with me, and for more time with them. What I have learned is that our children are not ours to keep. We protect them as long as we can, but ultimately, they are themselves and have to find their own way in life. I may not have been in close proximity geographically, but I believe she knew that I was emotionally always with her, never more than a phone call away.

I am grateful to have had this time with Cassie and to witness her conviction first-hand when she's had to do hard things. I've been by her side when she made unpopular choices and been the subject of others' negative judgements. I've watched her stand firmly and declare that she knows what is best for her. To this day, she continues to put herself first, something that took me decades to learn.

Love Triangle

I spent a week in Canada, negotiating the terms of Cassie's move with Jason. Dustin had been right; I was a lot harder to ignore in person than across an ocean.

I was on the front steps of their house three nights in a row. Each time, as my discussions with Jason wound down, I'd ask if he'd get Aidan to come see me. He'd go down the stairs and return, saying he was doing schoolwork or was already asleep. But I could see the light of his basement bedroom through the cracks of the blinds. I had to stop myself from crouching outside in the bushes and banging on his window until he showed his face.

I reached out to him several times during that week, offering to take him out for dinner or lunch, just the two of us. He declined all my invitations, texting to say he was too busy. I considered ambushing him at school. Luckily, my sanity returned before I acted on these impulses. I figured if I gave him space to process everything, he might come around. I also considered that, at fifteen, he might just be a broody teenage boy not interested in being seen in public with his mom. But he didn't change his mind. I was heartbroken that he and I didn't talk at all while I was there. I'd hoped we'd closed some distance while we were in Zurich, but now, standing on the front steps, he felt a million miles away.

By the time I flew back to Zurich, we had settled on a move date, I had a court-ordered change of custody in place, and we could start the visa application process. Cassie would remain in Canada for another few weeks, and then she would move. I had brought three empty suitcases with me and gave them to her. 'Pack everything you want in these,' I said. 'There's a chance that some of your stuff won't be there next time you visit Dad.'

Dustin and I flew to Canada to accompany Cassie on her one-way flight to Zurich. My parents insisted on seeing her off, too. It was important that we all be present for this grand moment. She had made the bold and unexpected decision to move away, and we wanted her to know that we were there to support her. Besides, by now I knew that there's strength in numbers. All the times I'd been ostracized, standing alone at the hockey arena, had taught me the importance of having people in your corner. We all need a tribe, a group who loves and supports us without judgment, during tough times and when we are vulnerable. I wanted that for Cassie on this momentous day.

I stared down the long hallway near security. Dustin checked his phone. She really should have been here by now. Surely Jason wouldn't derail the process?

I walked along the hallway, looking out the windows. I stopped and pressed my forehead against the cool glass. I closed my eyes and took a deep breath in. My exhale fogged up the glass and I drew a small heart. I looked at the time again. I turned to Dustin and he smiled. Suddenly I spotted them in the crowd of people. My heart skipped a beat. She was here. With all three suitcases I had brought for her. There was an awkward silence as we all stood in a semi-circle, careful not to cross invisible barriers. Cassie looked around quietly from Jason, to his mother, to me and to Dustin. The air was heavy. Dustin brought a trolley for the luggage.

'We should get these checked in,' he said. Cassie looked hesitantly towards Jason.

'You'll be able to say goodbye after we drop these off. It'll just be a few minutes,' I said and we followed Dustin into the lineup for baggage drop-off.

She was very quiet. I looked back. Two families standing a few feet apart from us had all eyes on us. I put my hand on her shoulder and asked if she was excited. She nodded slowly. Dustin shot me a look that said, 'Not now.' I let out a sigh. We handed the gate agent our passports and boarding passes. A few keystrokes and clicks of the mouse, and we were ready to go.

We said our goodbyes to my parents first. Cassie went to her Dad and Granny and said her goodbyes. The hugs were long and hard. I felt their sadness from where I was standing, but I didn't want to be drawn into it.

'I'll text you when we land. And I'll make sure to have her text or FaceTime you once she sets up her new phone,' I said to Jason. He nodded. I avoided making eye contact with his mom. I couldn't stand to see the grief in her eyes. All these years later, and I still wished she and I could have maintained some kind of a relationship. She had been a second mother to my kids since I moved away. She'd lost a daughter-in-law ten years ago, and now she was saying goodbye to her granddaughter.

Jason pulled Cassie in again and kissed the top of her head. 'Love you, Princess.' The airport was quiet. There was no lineup at security. Walking towards the agent, I felt the heaviness in Cassie's heart. She'd barely made eye contact with me since she arrived. I turned around and waved to my parents, and although they were sad, I could see the joy in their eyes that, this time, I was not alone. Cassie turned to wave to her dad and Granny, but they'd already started down the long hallway to the airport exit.

We found a restaurant near our gate where we ordered drinks and snacks, and Dustin proposed a toast. 'To new beginnings,' he said. Cassie looked up, a big smile on her face at last. 'To new beginnings.'

On the flight, we looked through materials for a school in Zurich. We started making plans for her integration. She was excited and chatty, ready to dive in. But every now and then, I caught a glimpse of her looking out the window with a forlorn look on her face, and I knew exactly what she was thinking.

Did I make the right decision?

Changes

I quickly silenced the alarm. I'd been awake for an hour, waiting for the sound that told me it was time. I felt Dustin get up and make his way to the bathroom. I quietly pulled my pants, shirt and slippers on and headed to the kitchen. I turned on the hood fan light so as not to blind myself and started my morning. It was a routine I knew so well I didn't even have to think; my body just moved rhythmically, like a dance I'd mastered. I felt a smile creep onto my lips. This was exactly where I wanted to be and, in this moment, I felt happy. My heart fluttered and my skin prickled. I packed lunches and made breakfast: French toast for her, fried egg and bagel for him.

    I heard the shower turn off, started the coffee machine, placed his banana, iPad and glasses on the breakfast bar. I put her multivitamin next to her water and made her a small coffee. She was probably too young for it, but she liked the taste. I heard the familiar crack of the bar stool as she plopped down on it, eyes half-opened, groaning at the thought of being up. She ate quickly and quietly, moving to the sofa for her after-breakfast fifteen-minute nap before getting ready for school, and I started washing the dishes. I finished right in time for her to get dressed.

'Mom, I don't know what to wear,' she called out, dragging herself to her room.

'Be right there,' I said, making a coffee and taking it to her room. She lay on her bed; morning had never been her thing. Together we decided on an outfit, and I coaxed her to get moving so we wouldn't be late for the train. The pups ran out of their crates looking for water, food and affection. She picked Blue up, hugged him tightly and then placed him on her bed. He automatically rolled over for belly rubs, and she indulged him.

She was finally ready, and we headed off to the train station. School bag, gym bag, lunch bag, tram pass, house keys—yes, we had everything. It was a cold morning, and we could see our breath as we spoke. She held out her elbow for me to link in my arm, and I accepted it willingly. We huddled a little closer, trying to create some warmth. I turned to Dustin, who was walking a few steps behind us, carrying some of her bags. With every step, she became more chatty and full of life. The cold had done its job, by the time we got to the train station, she would be completely alert.

'I just don't get it, Mah, how do you get Bill from William or, like, Dick from Richard?' she asked.

'I don't know kiddo, they just do,' I said, laughing at the randomness of our morning conversations. Her mind was constantly filled with a million haphazard thoughts. How did she ever focus at school?

We sent her off on the train to school and I saw Dustin off to his train to work. Walking back home, I smiled, thanking God and the Universe for finally giving me what I'd been praying for over so many years. She had been with us for a while now, and with every day that passed, we seemed to be getting closer. She was settling in at school and had made several friends. She liked the freedoms I afforded her but understood that I expected her to be completely honest with me at all times.

She brought so much joy to the apartment in which I used to feel so lonely. I loved having her around and relished my role as a full-time mother. We had dance-offs in the living room. I was teaching her how to make some of her favorite dishes and would sit at the kitchen table to help with her homework. She reminded me of myself as a young teenager, basking in the attention of my parents every chance I got. She was reveling in being the only child—the center of attention, because, for so many years, she had lived in her brother's shadow. She knew her dad loved her very much. But, just as I find it effortless to be with Cassie, Jason has a more natural affinity with our son. They bonded over videogames, ice hockey and sports, with him frequently coaching Aidan's teams. Inadvertently, this meant that Cassie had often been left behind, or was forced to tag along. She held no bitterness, though, for either one of us. She was wise beyond her years and already understood that life is never perfect.

I thought of Aidan every day and wondered what he was up to. I kept telling myself that in time, he might come around and want to reconnect with me. You would think that after everything, I'd have learned to accept life as it is instead of continually wanting more. But he is also my child. And I couldn't let go of my longing for a relationship with him. Sometimes, I'd remind myself not to be so consumed by Aidan's ghosting of me, so as not to leave Cassie feeling that she was still stuck in his shadow.

But in the privacy of my thoughts, I still longed for my son, even as I gave thanks for the return of my sweet girl.

Silence

When did I lose him? I keep asking myself.

We had started drifting apart after I left Jason, and more so once he approached that magical age of twelve, when he would be able to negotiate his visits. I can understand his hurt and sadness.

But even in my worst moments, I never imagined I would lose him completely.

Over the years, I wrote him letters and long text messages and prayed for a few words in return, small crumbs I could clutch to my heart. But eventually all his responses dried up completely and a silence crept in between us. It became deafening when he sent me his last message—a few short sentences, asking that I stop trying to communicate with him, informing me that he no longer wanted me to be part of his life. I read and reread the words, willing them to change. I scrolled through all the messages I had sent him, trying to find the exact moment where it all broke down. Maybe if I could find it, I could fix it.

On our first New Year's Eve in Zurich, Cassie and I made a video of the fireworks from the Zurich lakefront and sent it to him, wishing him a happy new year. I thought he'd want to see that his sister was doing well and adjusting to her new life. Maybe if he saw that she was happy, it would make him happy, too, and he might reconsider his decision and want to be part of my life, now that she was with me. I fantasized that she might be the bridge to reconnect us. It never occurred to me how damaging this might be for her. I should never have psychically roped her in to help save my relationship with her brother. It took a while for me to appreciate what an unfair weight this placed on her shoulders. Even as I was doing it, I couldn't see it.

It was a gray morning when I walked up the stairs from the tramline with the groceries. I went straight from walking Cassie to the train station to the grocery store, planning to lock myself in for the rest of the day. I looked at the clock while I put away the groceries. It was the middle of the night where he was. I should wait to send a message. I didn't want to wake him up. Although he would probably have his phone on silent. And, well, he hadn't responded to the last dozen I'd sent. I sat at my desk to write and instead stared out the window onto the lake. I'd been trying to write him a letter for weeks now. I never knew what to say. Most days, I didn't get past 'Dear A, how have you been? I miss you so much,' before deleting the words.

I looked at the clock again. Almost noon here. He would be getting up and ready for school soon. I picked up my phone and opened the Messenger app. I tapped on his name. His smiling face was in a tiny circle on the left. I stared at it and smiled, feeling a pang in my heart.

I typed a short message: *Hey kiddo, hope you have a great day at school. Think about you often and miss you lots. Let's talk soon, ok? Love ya.*

I pressed send. Maybe this time he would respond. I put the phone on silent and placed it on the desk. I logged into my writing class website and got to work. Out of the corner of my eye, I saw my phone screen light up. I quickly picked it up, praying it was a response from him.

New Message from Dustin: *Hey, babe, how's your morning? Looks like the sun wants to come out.*

I replied: *Good. Just working on my writing. How 'bout you?*

New Message from Dustin: *Busy. You should take the pups for a walk today. Take advantage of the nice weather.*

I replied: *I was planning on it. See you tonight. Love you.*

I cleaned the dishes as I stared out the window. It was a beautiful sunny afternoon. I checked my phone. No new messages. In the bedroom I closed the blinds so that the room was completely dark. I lay on the bed and set my alarm for 3 p.m. Enough time to pull myself together before Cassie got back from school. I wrapped the blankets tightly around my body and sank into the cold silence.

In these dark months after Aidan's last message, I had become frozen with grief, replaying all the conversations we'd had during his seventeen days in Zurich. I was stuck in ambiguous loss, unable to accept his decision. Whenever I found myself alone, I would drown in the deep sorrow of losing him. Instead of honoring his wish, I continued to send him message after message, hoping he would respond.

•••

I became so hung up at having no relationship with Aidan that I began to damage the one I had with Cassie. I was blind to her pain and loss, because I was so focused on my own. I pulled away from her and Dustin and wallowed in self-pity. I wasted time regretting what I didn't have, instead of being grateful for what I did. I needed to believe he'd been manipulated to feel and think about me the way he did and that he was being forced into have no contact with me, to show his loyalty to his father. That was far easier than accepting the alternative. I wanted so badly to believe that Jason was the villain and had poisoned Aidan against me that I could not accept that, perhaps, my son had made up his own mind that he didn't want anything to do with me.

Positively Complicated

Even though she had been living with us for four months, every time I'd open the door to check on her, I half-expected to see the bed empty, and to find that I had dreamed her moving to live with us. The moonlight shone softly on her angelic face. She had changed so much over the years, yet when she was asleep, she still looked like her three-year-old self. Tangled up in the blankets, curls all around her face, she would grind her teeth when she slept. My heart broke a bit, even though she was here now. All those times I'd missed out on weighed on me so heavily, it felt like I was drowning. I closed my eyes, took a deep breath and shut the door. I couldn't continue to focus on the past, I told myself; it wouldn't do anyone any good. All I could do was make the best of the time we had now.

The next day, she arrived home from school, bubbly and chatty. She pulled a sheet out of her bag and showed me that she got an A on her Humanities exam. Heading to her room, she asked me to put the sheet back in her binder. Not wanting it to fold or rip, I pulled everything out of her bag and noticed an English assignment titled 'My Scrambling Biography.' I started to read it. As I did, I felt as if I'd been punched in the gut.

She wrote of being extremely homesick, and how no place other than her dad's would ever be 'home'; of how she missed the smell of her Granny's apple pies, raspberry scones and macaroons; that her decision to move to Zurich was made on an impulse, 'because I was angry.'

I continued reading, even as my heart clattered in my chest. I learned that she 'can't wait to go back home for the summer and laugh with my father, brother, grandparents and cousins; my family.'

Were we not her family, too? Could she not laugh with us? My heart was in a million pieces. The only small comfort I could take was her last sentence: 'BUT I don't regret it.'

In all this time, I had thought that she was adjusting to her new school, making friends, growing roots. How could I have been so blind?

I wondered if she'd written these words to get them out of her head and heart? To lay them bare on the page? Was this a shitty first draft that no one was ever meant to read?

Later, I knocked on her door. I didn't tell her I'd read her Scrambling Biography, but I let her know that I'd noticed she hadn't spoken to her dad and the family she'd left behind for some months. Was it because she missed them too much?

'Maybe.'

'Do you want to go back to Dad's?'

'No, I want to stay.'

She asked me to leave her room and slammed the door behind me, irate.

Maybe I wasn't supposed to read her essay. Or perhaps she had left it knowing I would, and this was her way of telling me what she was feeling without having to look me in the eyes.

I sat at the kitchen table, trying to make sense of it all, and then the knowing part of me whispered softly: *Remember all the times you started over?* Every life decision I'd made had been on an impulse, inspired by a spark in my heart saying, *this is what I want*, and the decision was made before my brain could stop it. I reminded myself that I couldn't force her to consider Zurich her home. I couldn't stop her from missing the life she had before she came to live with me. I couldn't erase the memories, laughter and good times she'd had. They were hers to keep, and I shouldn't want her to forget them. She was here with me. And that was more than enough.

I was learning to live in a world where her past, present and future could hold both her father and me. I was beginning to understand that there was enough space in her heart for all of us to coexist.

The Irony of Life

Cassie had been living with us for three months, and we still didn't have her visa. Dustin came home from work early one night, and he wasn't smiling. There was a knot in my stomach when he motioned to the bedroom door.

He closed the door quietly. 'We got rejected,' he said, turning to face me.

I fiddled with my hands in my lap. 'What? What do you mean?'

'Cassie. Her visa. The application got rejected.' He sat down next to me.

'No, no, babe. The immigration person said we would get it.' I didn't want to believe him.

He wiped a tear from my eye. 'I'm so sorry. They don't know what happened.'

'But she's here. She can't go back.' Suddenly I couldn't breathe. 'No, we can't send her back. I can't do that. I can't choose again.'

'Babe, you're not choosing. What do you mean, choosing?'

'I can't choose between you and her. I can't make that choice again.' Memories flashed in my mind of past decisions.

'You don't have to choose, Sonia. She's with us. We're in this together. The three of us.' He stood and pulled me towards him. We held each other, letting the enormity of this terrible news sink in. We both agreed not to tell Cassie anything while we appealed the decision. There was no point in worrying her unnecessarily.

We filed our formal appeal two weeks later. Our case would be reviewed by an immigration officer within the Appeals Division. An immigration officer on a different floor of the same building. 'But it's a very transparent process,' we were assured by the person handling her visa application.

We also filed an informal appeal, requesting that the original officer and his team leader revisit their decision based on additional information we sent in. Within a few days, we were advised that they had reviewed the additional information, but the original decision remained unchanged. Her visa application was denied.

Our immigration lawyer recommended we put Cassie through a psychological assessment. 'It might help us demonstrate that there were underlying issues in Canada and that it is in her best interest to live with you.'

We received a letter from the Appeals Division stating that Cassie could remain in Switzerland while they reviewed the case. However, if she left the country, she would be denied re-entry. We had no choice but to tell her about the rejection. It was difficult to break the news that, in the interim, she wouldn't be able to visit her dad. And that she'd have to see a psychologist.

'Okay, so what does it mean?' she asked, looking from me to Dustin.

'Well, for now it just means that you can't leave Switzerland,' Dustin explained.

'But for how long?' The disappointment was evident in her body.

'We're not sure, kiddo. Hopefully we get an approval in the next few weeks and everything's good.'

'And the psychologist? How long do I have to do that for?'

'Only for a few sessions. Two or three. She'll do some standardized tests and talk to you about living with Dad. We just have to demonstrate that it's better for you to live with us.'

'Will I have to talk about Dad?'

'Probably. I think she'll ask about what it was like living with him. And you'll have to talk about me and DJ. She'll want to know why you wanted to move after being with Dad all that time.' She nodded.

I squeezed her hand. 'Like I said, kiddo, it's just a way to show that you being here is the best place for you. And if a Swiss-German psychologist says it is, well shit, then it must be true.'

She laughed. 'Okay, I'll do it.'

We continued living our lives while we waited. Dustin worked. Cassie threw herself into her schoolwork. The teachers told us she was adjusting very well. I took her to the psychologist. We all tried to ignore the looming threat that, at any given moment, we could be told that she had to leave, that we'd all have to leave. Knowing we might have to relocate, we wrote a list of possible places we might want to live on a piece of paper, and I tucked it away in a drawer. I didn't want to give too much energy to the prospect of relocating, as I firmly believe our thoughts create our reality.

A few months later, our appeal was denied, once again, on the same grounds. We had thirty days to file an appeal to the Federal Court. We decided to take a chance before a judge. Surely a judge would rule in our favor after reviewing the facts? We met with a new law firm specializing in immigration cases like ours. We sat across from each other at a long, glass table with bottles of sparkling water on a beautiful wooden tray.

'The biggest issue is that you did not apply for Cassie's visa within twelve months of your arrival in the country. Which would be fine if she was under the age of twelve,' the senior lawyer explained.

'I understand that, but we applied as soon as we were awarded custody from the Canadian court system.' I looked from one lawyer to the other. 'We needed to wait for that to apply.'

'We applied less than three months after her thirteenth birthday. Surely there has to be some leeway?' Dustin asked.

'We will do our best to ensure that all aspects of your case are taken into consideration. We've seen many cases like these, and we feel strongly that her application should have been approved right away. Unfortunately, the Swiss Immigration Office can be difficult.' The lawyer tapped the letter we brought with us. 'Which is exactly what they are doing here. They are not looking at the human aspect of this case; they are hiding behind the legislation. They do have wiggle room. What we want to do is really amplify the emotional reasons why your daughter should remain within your custody.'

I felt emboldened by her confidence as we shook hands and left. I spent the next few days writing out timelines and sent the law firm all the details they needed to put a strong case together for us. Cassie underwent another round of psychological assessments. More stress. More litigation fees. More worries. My biggest fear remained that, any day, she might turn to me and say, 'It's okay, Mah, I'll just go back to Canada.' It was so much to ask of a teenage girl—to be put through such scrutiny and under such stress. Thirty days later, we filed our appeal to the Federal Administrative Court.

Summer went by. We travelled through Switzerland. We went to the lake every weekend and took out paddleboards. We played tennis. We roamed around the old town, enjoying lunch on patios. I told Jason we were still waiting on Cassie's visa and that she couldn't travel until we had secured it. I omitted to tell him that the application had been rejected three times over and he didn't ask about it again. By now, Cassie's relationship with him was fraught. She had barely communicated with her dad or brother since she'd moved. I tried to gently nudge her to reach out to them, for a call or a FaceTime, but she was unsure how it would all unfold because so much time had passed since their last goodbye. I'd remind her often that, no matter what had happened or how much time went by, they all loved her very much and it would not be weird to talk with them. I didn't press her, because I knew she was already carrying a heavy burden of not knowing when and how our lives might have to change.

August rolled around and Cassie started school again—Grade 9, high school.

It was in late September that we received an email from the immigration law firm. It had been a few months since we submitted our appeal to the Federal Administrative Court. They had warned us that it could take a while to get a response. 'It all depends on the case load. And the court closes for August holidays.'

I tapped to open the email: *We are very sorry ... we wish we had better news ... has been denied ... please call us at your earli—*

The phone slipped out of my hands and hit the ground. I sat, shaking. No. No, no, no, no. This couldn't be happening. I couldn't lose her again.

I called Dustin.

'Hey babe, how's your—'

'Did you see the email?' I interrupted him.

'What? No, I've been in meetings all morning. I haven't been at my desk.'

'Check your emails. We got another rejection.' I heard him clicking. I could hear him mumbling as he read it. 'I'll call the lawyer now and call you back.'

I was numb. As I waited for Dustin to call me back, I wondered, why? Was I being punished for not trying harder to hold onto my children the first time around? Was this karma, coming back to bite me in the ass? Was I not meant to be a mother?

Dustin called to tell me that we had a meeting with the lawyers the following Monday.

'They want to go over our options.'

We agreed not to say anything to Cassie until we knew more. I spent the afternoon running the letter from the Federal Administrative Court through Google Translate. All official correspondence had been sent to us in German, and neither of us was fluent. I could make out bits and pieces— that they agreed that the original decision was the right one.

I couldn't believe that this was happening. I stood on the terrace, watching for the tram that she usually caught home. I watched her step off and cross the street with her friend. Walking into the apartment she asked, 'Can I go with Julia to their cottage in Flims for the weekend?'

'Did you run this by your mom?' I asked Julia.

'Yes. She said that she would text you. It will be just us three. My dad and sister are staying home.'

'Alright, sure. You should get packing, then. Don't forget to bring your schoolwork with you.' It was probably better for Cassie to be away for the weekend so Dustin and I wouldn't have to tiptoe around her while we had to keep this news from her.

Back at the lawyer's office the following Monday, the air was heavy. The junior lawyer began. 'We are deeply sorry about this decision. We are so confused at the outcome. We truly expected that it would come out in your favor.' Her sympathetic tone irritated me.

'What can we do? What are our options?' I asked.

'Well, as I said to your husband last Friday, you have very limited options.' The senior lawyer tapped the papers in front on her. Our file. It was thick. 'The Federal Administrative Court is siding with the earlier decisions. They are sticking to the application timeline issue. They have looked at the other evidence we provided and do not feel that it is compelling enough to go against the clear immigration laws.'

'I thought I read something about 'Oktober zuerst' in the document. Does this mean that we have to leave by October 31st?' I asked.

'It means that Cassie has to leave Switzerland by October 31st.'

'That's in five weeks,' I said. 'How are we supposed to leave the country in five weeks?'

'We do have one more recourse that could buy you some time. We can appeal to the Supreme Court. We would likely not win, but it might give you a little bit more time to plan for your next step.'

I looked at Dustin. 'Would Cassie be able to stay during this process?' he asked.

'We would have to make a special request to the Court but cannot be certain that they would approve this request. She has already been in the country without a visa for almost a year.'

I looked at my hands in my lap. 'Okay. We will let you know our decision soon.' I stared out the window.

In that moment, I found myself back on the front stoop of my old marital home with a garbage bag of my belongings at my feet. The memory of seeing my small children pushing and pulling at the baby gate at the top of the stairs, calling out for me, was vivid. I felt as helpless in this moment as I had back then. All I wanted was to have a chance at being a full-time mother. I wanted to witness my daughter growing and flourishing in this environment. I wanted to cheer her on as she became more and more confident in herself and in her accomplishments.

And now the Swiss Immigration Authority was trying to separate me from my daughter. I could not accept that someone who knew nothing about our lives, about everything we had been through for the past ten years, about how much I had fought to keep a close and loving bond with my daughter, could decide that it would be in her best interest to return to Canada. The lawyer's voice interrupted my thoughts and I blinked away my tears.

'Mrs. Lamarche, if you decide not to pursue to the Supreme Court, it is imperative that Cassie leave Switzerland by October 31st. Her passport will be flagged, and if she is not gone, the Polizei will come for her.'

We left the lawyer's office, stunned with uncertainty once again.

Houston Bound

We had kept Dustin's employer abreast of Cassie's visa issues from the start. They were supportive throughout the entire process. And when Dustin informed them of the latest rejection, they offered him a transfer to the Houston headquarters. We accepted the offer without hesitation and jumped into action. The countdown began again. We had thirty-five days to leave. I didn't bother with a calendar this time.

'Happy hour time, Cassie,' Dustin called out. I patted the cushion next to me. 'Come sit, kiddo, we have to talk to you.'

She hesitated before coming back in, sensing that this was not going to be a fun chat. 'So, we got some bad news last week, squirt. The court denied your visa application again. We met with the lawyers and there's nowhere else to appeal,' Dustin said.

'Is that where you went the other morning after dropping me off at the train station?'

'We didn't want to mention it until we heard what they had to say. We knew this could happen, right? That's why we made a list of where else we would want to live a couple of months ago.' She nodded.

'Well, my company has offered me a job in Houston. And, if I recall, we did have Houston on our list,' Dustin continued.

Her hand went up. 'Will I be able to finish my semester here?'

'I'm sorry, kiddo. We have to be gone by October 31st. After that, we'll get in trouble.'

She sighed. 'Well, will I be able to visit Dad at Christmas?'

'Yes. One hundred percent. You'll be able to come and go as you please.'

'Can I go back to my bedroom now?'

'Of course.'

'That went better than I thought it would,' he said after she left the room.

I nodded. 'I'm going to email Jason and tell him that your company is transferring us. I won't say anything about the visa.'

Over the following weeks, I readjusted to the news, trying to find the silver lining in yet another difficult situation. These rejections were a blow, and I'd struggled to figure out what the upside was. It was ironic—I had spent years hoping and praying that my kids would be with me full-time. Then, finally, Cassie had chosen to uproot herself completely, leaving the only life she had known behind. She was just settling in to her new normal when the governing authority decided it was in her best interests to return to her father in Canada. I admit, at the time, I felt as if I was being punished for not having been a better mother, for not having done more, or fighting harder in the past. I could not find a single positive aspect in this entire situation.

I've since changed my mind. Now I see that there was an order to it all. If we hadn't left Canada, Cassie would not have had the opportunity to make the choice to move to be with us and I would never have known that she would choose to spend her teenage years with me by her side. Perhaps the physical distance offered reasons other than, 'I want to live with Mom.' The chance of an education at an international school, travel opportunities, new life experiences and exposure to exciting cultures all weighed on the side of her choice, while minimizing the hurt left behind. It wasn't a choice between Mom or Dad; it was the prospect of exciting possibilities that living abroad could offer her.

Zurich had been good to us. Good to all three of us, but I wasn't sad to leave. I once thought that Zurich had tried to take Cassie away from me.

But, in the end, it actually brought her to me.

(Un)Settled

We landed in Houston on a stormy October 31st. Lightning. Thunder. Flash flooding. Apparently, that was normal here. Halloween was canceled for those who waited too long to go trick-or-treating. We sat on the runway, unable to de-plane until the storm had passed. At least we had managed to get Cassie out of Zurich in time. I still don't know how we got it all done—find housing in Houston, set up bank accounts, enroll Cassie in school, close everything in Zurich, pack and ship all our belongings. We had to fly through Canada to apply for our US visas. The process was seamless. When we handed our thick file to the immigration officer, I held my breath. Stamp, stamp, stamp. Please stand here, place your fingertips here. Okay, approved.

'Let's hurry in case they change their mind,' I whispered to Dustin.

It all took eighteen hours, two planes and three airports. We did it with nine suitcases, three carry-ons, and two small dogs. Here we were. Landing in yet another new chapter. Cassie was sleeping, her cheek resting on the plane window. I closed my eyes and listened to the thunder as lightning flashed under my eyelids. Two hours went by before we could finally enter the airport terminal. It was well after midnight by the time we checked into our hotel room. The car ride was a blur. Dustin opened the small bottle of champagne from the mini-fridge, poured two glasses and handed me one. He handed Cassie the cola bottle. The dogs stretched out, yawning. We raised our drinks, 'To new beginnings.'

Our sea shipment arrived a few days before she left for Christmas in Canada with her dad and brother. She hadn't seen them in over a year and had barely had any communication with them. I kept busy by unpacking. The house was cold and empty without her. I sent her a few messages, but she didn't respond. I automatically went to the dark place, thinking that Jason had confiscated her phone. Or that she'd changed her mind and didn't want to come back to us. It didn't dawn on me that maybe she was just focusing on being where she was. I found it so hard not to jump to worst-case-scenario conclusions every time she went back. I held my breath, almost expecting that she'd text me to say that it was all a big prank, that she actually didn't want to live with me. A part of me couldn't accept that she had chosen me. I was so used to rejection. Now that I had her, I was always worried I'd lose her or realize that she was never really with me. I can only imagine the burden she must have felt as I clung to her like a buoy. Whenever a wave of grief or sorrow threatened to pull me down and drown me, I dug my fingers into her more tightly. I made her my everything, and in doing so I forced her to help me carry my pain and anxieties. Now, whenever I find myself doing this, I close my eyes and imagine that she is a stream from the river of me and her father, and that my job is to let her current forge its own path.

We picked her up from the airport on New Year's Eve and grabbed pizza on the way home. I asked about her trip, but she didn't say much. I figured she was just tired and that she'd tell me more in the next few days. We watched the New Year's Eve Time Square special and, once the ball dropped, we all went to bed.

I turned the light off and snuggled into Dustin. 'Is it weird that she didn't really want to talk about her trip?'

'I don't know. Maybe. She's probably just tired.'

'Yeah, but she hasn't seen them in over a year. There had to have been some weirdness. I just hope that they didn't make her feel bad or anything.' He kissed the top of my head.

'I'm sure it was fine, babe. She can handle herself.'

•••

The following morning, we celebrated our Christmas. I sat with my coffee mug pressed against my lips and watched her unwrap her presents. 'So, what did Dad get you for Christmas, kiddo?' I asked.

She seemed irritated. 'Stuff.'

'What kind of stuff?' I pressed on. Dustin shot me a look over his glasses. 'Just stuff, Mah. I'll show you later, when I unpack.'

'And what about Aidan, did he get you anything?' Her eyes narrowed and she picked up her phone and started scrolling. I looked over to Dustin, sitting on the recliner with his iPad. I could feel my body tensing.

'Hey, do you have any pictures that you took while visiting? I'd love to see them,' I said, shifting in my seat. 'Kiddo, I'm talking to you.'

'I'm gonna go to my room,' she said, heading up the stairs.

I walked dejectedly to the kitchen, put my mug in the sink and leaned on the counter, looking out of the window. I shook my head, turned on the tap and started cleaning the dishes from breakfast. The warm water felt good on my hands. I felt the threat of tears and blinked them away.

I was so deeply absorbed in my loss, I couldn't seem to give Cassie the time and space she needed to process what she'd just experienced. It must have been a difficult trip for her. Or maybe it had gone so well that she'd realized she was happier with them and wanted to go back.

I heard Dustin behind me. 'You okay, babe?' I nodded, forcing a smile. He kissed me before heading for a shower.

When I heard it turn on, I let the hot tears fall.

Familiar Foe

We'd been in Houston for four months and were settling into a routine. I'd already made a few friends, which was more than I'd ever had in Zurich. Having only a one-hour time difference with our family made staying in touch easier. By this stage, I'd had zero communication with Aidan for almost two years. We were so close geographically, and yet the distance had never been greater. I scrolled through pictures and videos of him on my phone while Cassie was at school and Dustin was at work.

Every day I cried. There was a shakiness in my chest that I hadn't felt in a very long time. There was a hole in my heart I couldn't fill, and I recognized the dark, velvety voice of depression beckoning me once more. I remembered its whispers, the stories it fed me, inviting me to lie with it. I tried to resist. I exercised more, convinced that the endorphins would help. I spent more time outdoors, in nature, hoping the sun would burn this sadness out of me. I forced myself to meditate, although sitting on that pillow only amplified depression's voice until all I heard were the ways in which I'd failed my children.

I finally accepted I couldn't get through this on my own. I was honest with my doctor about my feelings. He explained that many women who have suffered from depression previously in life are likely to suffer again, especially when going through major hormonal changes. Thank you, perimenopause. He recommended a low dose of antidepressants and a heavy dose of talk-therapy. I left his office with my prescription in one hand and a thick handout of a list of psychologists covered by my insurance in the other.

How was I going to tell Dustin? I didn't want to worry him. He'd done everything he could to keep the three of us together. All he wanted was to see me happy. I felt hot shame for not being able to just keep it together. Standing in the bathroom, I opened the paper bag and pulled the yellow bottle out. Sertraline 100 mg. Half a pill a day. I opened the bottle and dumped one in my hand. I carefully broke it in half. I remembered standing by the kitchen sink years ago. Happy pills. *Mommy needs to take them because we don't make her happy anymore.*

I shook the memory away. This was not like last time. I'd been through postpartum depression and not only survived, but I'd experienced love and joy and peace afterwards. This gave me the strength to trust I would be okay this time, too. Staring at my reflection in the mirror, I filled up the glass with water. This was temporary. Just until I started to feel better. I looked at the pill in the palm of my hand and took a deep breath. I threw it in my mouth and swallowed it. I lay down on my bed. I set my clock for 3 p.m. Enough time to freshen up and put on a smile before Cassie got home.

Later, Dustin and I sat quietly in the backyard. The breeze felt humid on my skin. He asked about my appointment. 'The doctor thinks it's depression. Probably brought on by my perimenopause.'

'I know you haven't been feeling great lately, but I didn't think it was that bad,' he said, turning to face me.

'It is. I just haven't wanted to say anything. I guess I was embarrassed. I mean, look at me. Look at us, what do I have to be depressed about?' I said, trying to sound unruffled. I was good at pretending I had everything under control. I hid my emotions so well, Dustin hadn't realized how much I was struggling. I didn't want to burden him. And so instead I lied. Until I couldn't anymore.

Dustin saw through it. 'What does he recommend?'

'Happy pills. And therapy.' I gazed at the ground, feeling the heat rise to my cheeks.

He crouched in front of me, took my hands and looked deeply into my eyes. 'Hey, don't do that. Take the pills; they helped you last time. You're with me now. We're going to get through this.' He kissed my cheek and wiped away the tears.

All I was certain of was that this time wouldn't be anything like the last.

All those years ago, in the deepest pit of my postpartum depression, I had felt profound loneliness. I was isolated, lost in the deep, dense fog. I couldn't lean on my husband. I couldn't connect with my newborn baby, and all the love I had for my son somehow evaporated.

It's hard to explain depression to someone who's not lived through it. It never really goes away. It gets better—I get better. And life goes on. But I'm keenly aware that it follows me around like a shadow; that at any given time, it might catch up to me and we'll sit together at the edge of the abyss. I recognize it now, the tipping point, when I'm falling for depression's lies. And I know to pull myself away and ask for help.

As part of my healing, I have become more aware of the long and nefarious history of depression in my family. It has been courting us for generations. I shouldn't be surprised that I couldn't escape it. I remember my father grappling with his mother's mental illness. My child's eyes could see the darkness that followed my grandmother, how she was laden with heavy, oppressive energy. We all tiptoed around it, almost afraid it might stick to us if we got too close. Some years ago, my strong father, who rarely shows his feelings, was diagnosed with acute depressive disorder following a mental breakdown. The first time I heard him cry was when I was a child and his father had died, I had run away from the bathroom door, unable to accept that my father was crying. It had to be someone else. My dad didn't cry. At the time, I didn't have the capacity to hold space for his grief and sadness. I was only a child.

A few years ago, when my mother had to undergo open-heart surgery and we didn't know if she would make it, I held him as he wept in my arms. It was a moment in which he allowed himself to openly show me behavior he'd always considered a weakness. I understood then that he—like all of us—is broken, too. He is human and feels deeply. We are all broken in our own way. It helps us to know that we are not alone—that others suffer in the ways we do.

Depression splits you open. It tears you down and forces you to put yourself back together. Having a person you can lean on when you're in your darkest place can make all the difference. It's like having a guide waiting to lead you out of the fog.

I am blessed to have had Dustin by my side to help me find my way back.

If there's one thing I can thank Jason for, it's teaching me that there is strength and hope, in numbers.

Moving On

I've been seeing Dr. Max weekly for about two months now. Healing, he reminds me, is not a linear path. Rumination is the devil's tool. When you can't get out of your head, distract yourself. Your mind will play tricks on you. Sometimes, all the options are shitty, but you still have to pick one. These are some of the gems he throws my way during our sessions.

In our first session, he asked what I thought the biggest situational reason for my depression might be. 'My relationship with my son.' I paused. 'Actually, it's the lack of a relationship with my son.' So we have spent a lot of time talking about Aidan.

I am sitting in the waiting room when Dr. Max opens the door. 'Sonia,' he says, smiling as he sweeps his hand, inviting me in.

I walk to his office at the end of the hallway and take my usual seat in the corner of the oversized sofa. I wonder if it would be comfortable to lie on.

'What can I do for you today?' he asks as he glances over my file.

I look down at my hands in my lap. 'Well, I wrote that letter for Aidan, like you suggested.'

'Would you like to share it with me?' I nod and pull it out of my purse. I read it aloud to him, the words blurred through my watering eyes.

'I think I've made my peace and am ready to let go. I'm going to handwrite it and put it in a card. His birthday is coming up on the 28th,' I say.

'Oh, very good. The timing works, especially given the contents of the letter.' He looks at me and puts my file on the arm of his recliner. 'How does it make you feel? To send it, not knowing how he will react or if he will even read it?'

'Like a kick in the teeth. I hate that it's come to this.'

'Come to what?'

'Come to the point that I have no relationship with him.'

He picks up my file and peruses it, clicking his pen. 'From what we've discussed in our sessions, this isn't a new thing. You've had a strained relationship with him for years. The development is that, some time ago, he specifically told you that he no longer wanted to speak to you or hear from you.'

I feel like I've been punched in the face. 'Hmmm. True.' I look out the window. Dr. Max is waiting for me to go on. I sigh. 'I know that this is what he wants. And I need to accept that he is old enough to make such a decision. I know, by not honoring it for the last year, I've done the exact opposite of what he wants. But I miss him.'

'Who do you miss?' he says, waving his hand. 'Which version of Aidan is it that you miss?'

'Him. I miss the Aidan that would give me the tightest hugs. The one that always had to be close to me. I miss his big blue eyes and how long his lashes looked on his cheeks when he slept in my lap. I miss my boy.'

'I understand.' He pauses and clicks his pen. 'That Aidan doesn't exist anymore.'

I swallow hard. His eyes burn through me. I don't like what he's saying. I clench my jaw and look at him. His eyes are soft and he tilts his head to the left. 'Do you understand that? Do you understand that the Aidan you miss isn't real anymore? That version of him no longer exists.'

I bite the inside of my lower lip to prevent myself from crying. I want him to stop talking. But he continues. 'The Aidan that exists now, is a sixteen-, soon to be seventeen-year-old young man. And this young man has specifically requested that you stay out of his life until he is ready to let you back in. And, if and when this happens, he won't be the Aidan that you remember; he will be who he is at that time.'

My lower lip starts to quiver, and I blink hard.

'Now, I understand that you miss him, and that is absolutely normal. You miss the memory of Aidan, you miss who he used to be. No one remains who they were. We all change. We all grow, and the sooner you can accept that the Aidan you yearn for no longer exists, the easier it will be for you to accept and respect his wishes.'

'Okay,' I say weakly.

'Okay,' he repeats. We shake hands and I leave his office.

The next afternoon, I walk down to the post office. It's a breezy spring day; the Houston humidity hasn't set in yet. I hand the letter to the person at the counter.

'Do you want a tracking number for this?' he asks.

I hesitate. 'No, thank you.'

On the way out, I toss the receipt into a garbage bin, look up at the sky and smile. I put my headphones on and start to walk home. Stopping by a lilac tree, I break a small branch and bring the blooms to my nose, inhaling deeply. The scent of lilac has always filled my heart with stillness.

I check my watch. Cassie will be back from school soon.

Maybe I'll take her out to Starbucks for an iced coffee and a brownie.

Acknowledgments

As a little girl, words were a lifeline for me and I dreamed of one day writing a book. I started writing my memoir, having no idea how much work it would be or how long it would take to complete. There are so many layers to work through, and I was fortunate enough to have the support of a wonderful group of people. I want to take a moment to thank each one of them for helping me achieve this monumental goal.

A huge thank you to my writing mentor and editor, Joanne Fedler, for seeing something in my writing and believing in me. Without your support and guidance, this book would not be the same. You pushed me to dig deeper, go past my fears and find my writing voice. Please know that you have not only helped me grow as a writer, you have helped me grow as a person.

To my Pod buddies from the Write your First Draft Masterclass, Susan and Alex: thank you for allowing me a safe space to be vulnerable and share my raw material. Your feedback, your support and your encouragement gave me the drive to keep writing.

To my fellow authors from the Sisterhood of the Rewrite, Lisa, Anna and Barbara: your generosity of time, support and feedback, coupled with your unwavering belief that I had an important story to tell and that it should be shared with the world, helped me keep the course. Thank you all so very much.

Thanks to my wonderful friends, Linda and Erin, for reading early drafts and encouraging me to keep writing.

Mom and Dad, thank you for giving me life and loving me unconditionally through all my ups and downs. Thank you for giving me permission to share not only my story but parts of yours as well.

To my kids, my love for you is eternal. Thank you for choosing me as your mother.

To my husband, my rock, my partner in life. Thank you for being the calm in my storms and for continuing to encourage me to pursue my dreams. You believe in me even when I don't.

To Brooke Shields, thank you for writing a book about a topic that no one really dared bring to the light. *Down Came the Rain* gave me the words I needed to express the pain and suffering I was going through. Your resilience and grace gave me the courage to believe that I could survive postpartum depression.

And lastly, thank you to everyone who reads my book. I hope that my story helps you in your own journey to finding peace in your life.

Author Biography

Sonia Lamarche grew up in a small Franco Ontarian town dreaming of a big city life. After living and working in various cities throughout Canada, Switzerland and Texas, Sonia considers herself an expert mover. She loves to read, write, cook and laugh and is obsessed with her Peloton exercise bike. She's recently returned to her Canadian small-town roots and currently resides in rural Nova Scotia with her husband, teenage daughter, two Chihuahuas and two black cats. She hopes to one day convince her husband that they need a few more cats.

www.ingramcontent.com/pod-product-compliance
Lightning Source LLC
Chambersburg PA
CBHW021434080526
44588CB00009B/521